THE MYTHMAKER

T0190604

The Mythmaker

A STUDY OF MOTIF AND SYMBOL IN THE
SHORT STORIES OF JORGE LUIS BORGES

BY CARTER WHEELOCK

UNIVERSITY OF TEXAS PRESS • AUSTIN

Requests for permission to reproduce material from
this work should be sent to:
    Permissions
    University of Texas Press
    P.O. Box 7819
    Austin, TX 78713-7819
    http://utpress.utexas.edu/index.php/rp-form

Library of Congress Catalog Number 76-102929

ISBN 978-0-292-72716-8, paperback
ISBN 978-0-292-78527-4, library e-book
ISBN 978-0-292-78570-0, individual e-book

For Ernestine

PREFACE

In this book I try to illustrate a fundamental—perhaps the most fundamental—aspect of the prose fiction of Jorge Luis Borges. It is one which gives unity to all of his best-known fictional work. An understanding of it greatly enriches, I think, a reader's experience of Borges' astonishing, profound, humorous, and disconcerting world of fantasy.

I believe that Borges' lasting fame in literature will come from the unique and superlative technology that characterizes his artistic expression of an essentially Baroque esthetic and of an idealism that is radical in our time but will perhaps be commonplace on some future day. Because of this I do not consider that this amazing author's work can be in any way impoverished by critical efforts to discover his patterns, his system, his linguistic techniques, and his semantic sleight-of-hand: that is, his superb artistry. I have written this book in the conviction that if it contributes anything to an understanding of Borges, it will contribute as much to a richer appreciation of his unique genius.

NOTE

Frequent parenthetical references to Borges' works are made in this book. The following abbreviations are used to refer to the original works in Spanish: A, *El Aleph*; AP, *Antología personal*; F, *Ficciones*; H, *El hacedor*; HE, *Historia de la eternidad*; I, *Inquisiciones*; OI, *Otras inquisiciones*; M, *Manual de zoología fantástica*. Where possible I will also refer the reader to the same material in a readily available English translation, as follows: *Fic.*, *Ficciones* (edited by Anthony Kerrigan); *Lab.*, *Labyrinths* (edited by Donald A. Yates and James E. Irby); *Dream.*, *Dreamtigers* (translated by Mildred Boyer and Harold Morland); *Oth. Inq.*, *Other Inquisitions* (translated by Ruth L. C. Simms); *Per.*, *Personal Anthology* (edited by Anthony Kerrigan).

Quotations from Borges are given in English, and the translations are mine; again, I indicate the location of the material in an English translation where possible. The critical reader will notice that my translations are inclined to be literal and technical; this is because I think it is important to preserve certain connotations or etymological nuances. For example, Borges uses here and there the phrase "fuego sin luz." Because of the special significance of fire and light in his stories, I translate "fire without light" instead of "invisible fire" (*Lab.*, 155) or "lightless fire" (*Lab.*, 143).

CONTENTS

THE MYTHMAKER

Borges, Symbolism, and the Esthetic Phenomenon

JORGE LUIS BORGES makes strange and compelling word-music. He plays only one instrument—the intellectual, the epistemological—but the strumming of his cerebral guitar sets into vibration all the strings of emotion, intuition, and esthetic longing that are common to sentient humanity. In his short stories alone he has written a symphony of the human consciousness—unfinished, not because he has left it incomplete, but because he sees human thought as unconsummated. Men may possibly have truth, his fictions tell us, and they can believe they have it, but they cannot know they have it. Tantalized by truth, they juggle their thoughts and words and haply achieve the dazzling suggestion of the imminence of a revelation. On this Borges has based his "esthetic of the intelligence."[1]

The idealist notion that human thought can attain only to a practical delusion or a cogent intuition casts virtually the same silhouette as the French Symbolists' concept of literary creation. Just as a Symbolist poem evokes an esthetic reality without naming it, by piling up its symbols and inklings, so does human thought seem to brush the hem of truth's garment without really possessing it full-bodied and warm. To name a thing, said Valéry, is to kill it, to reduce it from a live presence to a dead memory whose corpse is denotative language, distorted and desiccated. Mallarmé dreamed of a wordless poem.

The era of French Symbolism was a way station on the road to the recovery of a mythic outlook in literature. Borges was born there and became one of the few writers who finished the trip. He has a superb conceptual grasp of what Wilbur M. Urban has called "the natural metaphysic of the human mind"[2]—the abstracting, god-making, fluid, kaleidoscopic world view possessed by primitive men for want of a body of sure and useful knowledge, and the view to which sophisticated men inevitably return when they despair of truth. This *philosophia perennis* formulates a circular, predestined universe, capricious and chaotic, capable of an infinite number of equally valid configurations; a world in which everything conceivable is true and where "false" can only mean "unthought." Borges looks upon modern men, with their fixed

[1] I take this phrase from Enrique Anderson Imbert, *Historia de la literatura hispanoamericana*, II, 268, where it is attributed to Borges.

[2] *Language and Reality*, pp. 685–729. "Natural metaphysic" is a term borrowed from Henri Bergson; the phenomenon it points to is dealt with also by Mircea Eliade, Alan Watts, and other writers on myth and language. Urban says it is a world view, Platonic, poetic in expression, metaphysical, and dependent on a substance-attribute concept of being. For my conception of it I lean also on Ernst Cassirer's *Language and Myth*, his *Essay on Man*, and his *The Philosophy of Symbolic Forms*, Vols. I and II, where it is made clear that the mind of archaic man is characterized by conceptual fluidity proportionate to the lack of fixed criteria of truth.

hierarchy of knowledge and an idea of being that differs radically from the loose cosmologies of their ancient forebears, as if they were a choral group that sings only one dogmatized song. Through a relentless distillation of language and idea he dissolves the structure of this dubious and domineering music, reducing it to the primal notes of the scale, which are capable of unlimited rearrangement. He then composes anew, and although we may not recognize or espouse his varied and fantastic *capricci,* we are at a loss to gainsay them. What Borges gives us is uncanny in the Freudian sense: untrue, but somehow true—or, as Plato said of his myths, they are not true but there is something like them that is true. It is in this sense that Adolfo Bioy Casares and Ana María Barrenechea have said that Borges' fantasies are more real than reality.[3] His stories suggest other ways of interrelating the parts of the universe, other ontologies that we have forgotten or have not yet made.

This is only to say that Borges is mythic. In the ancient myth-maker and the radical philosophical idealist the wheel comes full circle. Because both are lacking an overriding perspective or mental commitment, their worlds are in flux, and each momentary contour of thought is as valid as another. An idea's value to the consciousness is the criterion of its truth. Perhaps Susanne K. Langer, herself an idealist and skeptic, has best expressed the point in her *Feeling and Form,* p. 81:

The mark of a genuine myth is its power to impress its inventors as literal truth in the face of the strongest contrary evidence and in complete defiance of argument. It appears to be so sacred a truth that to ask in what sense it is true, or to call it a figure of speech, seems like frivolity. For it is a figure of *thought,* not merely of speech, and to destroy it is to destroy an idea in its pristine phase, just when it dawns on people. That is why mythic beliefs really are sacred. They are pregnant, and carry an unformulated idea.

[3] See Ana María Barrenechea, *La expresión de la irrealidad en la obra de Jorge Luis Borges,* p. 15 (*Borges the Labyrinth Maker,* p. 16), and Adolfo Bioy Casares, "Lettres et amitiés," *L'Herne* (Spring, 1964), p. 17.

This pregnancy or expectancy is present in Borges' stories, and because of it Enrique Anderson Imbert can say (*Literatura hispanoamericana,* II, 270) that although we do not believe Borges' sophisms, we take his stories seriously.

Borges' intellectual esthetic, expressed as the imminence of a revelation that never comes, seems to declare the affinity of myth and art, if not their effectual identity:

Music, the states of happiness, mythology, the faces that time has wrought, certain twilights and certain places, want to tell us something, or they told us something we ought not to have missed, or they are about to tell us something; this imminence of a revelation that does not come is, perhaps, the esthetic phenomenon (*OI,* 12; *Oth. Inq.,* 5).

And in Borges' view the esthetic phenomenon occurs through the breach of reality: "unreality, which is a prerequisite of art" (*F,* 162; *Lab.,* 91; *Fic.,* 146); "in the beginning of literature is myth, and likewise in the end" (*H,* 38; *Dream.,* 42).

Borges does not pretend, and we do not expect, that some ultimate, objective revelation will really spring from his dissolution and reformation of reality; the symphony can never be finished. But it can be played infinitely. Meaning, beauty, and satisfaction lie in the crescendo that culminates in climactic moments of near-fulfil-ment, when a Name seems about to be called, a summary note struck, and the face of Truth revealed. But the revelation cannot come; life lies in illusion, said Schiller, and knowledge must be death. With the utterance of the hundredth name of God, with the final entrance of the aspiring student into the august presence of the long-sought, never-seen personage Almotásim, with the speaking of the poem that summarizes and eliminates the labyrinth of the king, with the death of Martín Fierro on a plain that is "about to say something," the ambiguous music—the universe as our esthetic dream conceived it—is fulminated.

It seems to me that this esthetic is central in many of Borges' stories, not only as a literary achievement but also as a theme or motif. He develops plots and imagery that depict its conceptual form, without purporting to lead us through the esthetic experience itself. I would maintain that he does indeed lead us through it, at least after we have overcome our first astonishment at his fictions, but he indicates that he thinks otherwise, as I shall show. He does not suppose, apparently, that in reading his tales we are going to lose ourselves in the mood or the action; instead, he gives us, with deceptive and very deliberate casualness, the symbols of an idea. Through his symbols and images he repetitiously and systematically *alludes*, and his allusions comprise much, if not most, of the real substance of his narratives. The semantic payload is given largely by suggestion.

In Borges' stories, where plural men are really one ("The Theologians"), where men kill each other by overt geometric design ("Death and the Compass") or esoterically by the rules of rhetoric ("Emma Zunz"), where they disappear on looking into mirrors ("Averroes' Search"), create other men by dreaming them ("The Circular Ruins"), or see the universe under a stair ("The Aleph"), fantasy is orderly and controlled. Each of these unusual occurrences is justified by sophistry. This is to say that Borges is not talking about the soluble fish of Dada, nor is he following willy-nilly a trail of correspondences that leads him beyond rationality without his having foreseen it. There is nothing in his erudite prose to suggest wild, dreamlike disorder, nor is there in fact anything suggesting his actual participation in the faith—the hope of discovery—that characterizes the French Symbolists and their successors, although there is much in his work to indicate his affinity for the theories of Valéry. His "imminence of a revelation" could be said to describe the artistic effect sought by the Symbolists; but that is just the point: he gives us an artistic description of an effect that he does not pretend to bring about. In the prologue to his *Personal Anthology* Borges cites passages from poems by Valéry and Tennyson and then comments that these passages "reproduce a mental process." He adds: "Once I also sought expression; now I know that my gods concede to me nothing more than allusion or mention" (*AP*, 7–8; *Per.*, *ix–x*). I think it is safe to take Borges seriously here (he is so often full of mischief and tricks, especially in his prologues and in interviews) and to assume that for him literary creation equates to the reproduction of a mental process; and, moreover, that in his works he modestly believes he has achieved only allusion to that process which others have reproduced. By "reproduce," obviously, he means "to produce anew," not merely to copy or reflect.

Borges' modesty is not justified by his works. Having to do with creation as such, many of his fictions comprise a literature about literature—art about art. Enthusiasts could say with considerable justification that Borges has encompassed or preempted the Symbolist-surrealist creators by taking their creative process as his very motif—or rather, he subsumes that process under a vaster idea of mental creation that transcends all expressive forms, for even when he is symbolizing or alluding to literary creation he is really talking about thought. Idealist philosophy does not play second fiddle to literary theory in his short stories. Remarkable and notorious is his detachment from every conventional literary theory and his appreciation of them all, and this fact is radically idealist and peculiarly mythic. Borges' stories in the aggregate comprehend, almost omnisciently, the abstract forms of literature and of its creation and its manner of being. It is almost as if Borges had uttered the hundredth word, calling the summational Name of literature; but, courteously, he speaks it obliquely, as if to spare literature the humiliation of fulmination.

It is for this reason that Borges is rightly called a Baroque writer. The Baroque is, essentially, a time or a circumstance in which the creative intellect ceases to find value in the results of thought and turns to contemplating the form of its own activity. The Symbolists were half-formed idealists groping on the brink of a new Baroque era. Having despaired of literal language, which kills reality, they nevertheless were still hopeful about the power of language-as-symbol. "Seers" and "artists" alike were still optimists, hoping to discover truth by feeling its effective presence in the hollow place at the middle of the surrounding images. While Borges sees their evocation of reality-as-ambiguity and their rising to the "timeless moment" as being the experience of the esthetic phenomenon ("el hecho estético"), he knows that this nameless reality and this mystical absorption into the universe are also illusions, metaphors, like language itself.[4]

Critics allude now and then to what they consider to be Borges' depiction of the arrival at transcending knowledge, or at what Barrenechea calls nihilism or pantheism.[5] The point is important enough to bear refinement. Marcel Raymond describes (in *From Baudelaire to Surrealism*, pp. 7–8) a kind of mystical transcendence which poets may experience (in this case Jean-Jacques Rousseau), and his words are all but a paraphrase of Tzinacán's experience in Borges' "The Writing of the God." The quotations, we are told, are from the Fifth Promenade of Rousseau's *Reveries*:

. . . "The sound of the waves and the agitation of the water," the tide and ebb, produce a rhythm that is no longer distinguished from that of. the heart, of the blood. But soon Narcissus, withdrawn into himself, no longer even desires to see himself; only the confused and delicious sense of existence survives in his ecstasy. "What does one enjoy in such a situation? Nothing outside oneself, nothing except oneself and one's own existence; so long as this state endures, one is self-sufficient like God." For opposition to the world has been renounced, and the self can no longer be distinguished from the cosmos. It is a natural mystical experience.

---

[4] In December, 1961, I asked Borges whether an allusion to "metaphors and seeming metaphors" implied a belief on his part that a true metaphor opens up a new level of reality. He replied: "I don't believe it is possible to open up a new level of reality. Back in the twenties some of my friends and I used to think so, but I don't think so any more." Cf. *OI*, 71; *Oth. Inq.*, 47.

[5] Barrenechea, *Expresión*, pp. 86–95 *passim; Borges the Labyrinth Maker*, pp. 87–97.

Compare the words of Tzinacán, alone in his dark prison:

Then occurred the union with the divinity, with the universe. . . . I saw an enormous wheel, which was not before my eyes, nor behind, nor at the sides, but everywhere at once. . . . I saw the universe and I saw the intimate purposes of the universe. . . . I saw the faceless god behind the gods. I saw infinite processes which formed a single happiness (A, 120).

And having divined the meaning of the secret inscription of the god, he adds:

The mystery that is written on the tigers, let it die with me. One who has glimpsed the universe, one who has glimpsed the burning designs of the universe, cannot think about one man, about his fortunes or mis-adventures, although that man be he. That man has been he and is now nobody. That is why I do not pronounce the formula, that is why I let the days forget me (A, 121).

What Raymond describes is like Valéry's experience in "The Marine Cemetery," and one immediately remembers André Mau-rois' observation that Borges "is akin to Kafka, Poe, sometimes to Henry James and Wells, always to Valéry" ("Preface" to *Laby-rinths,* eds. Yates and Irby, p. *x*). Perhaps Rousseau's or Valéry's mystical experience of self-loss is the same as Tzinacán's; but the former is essentially intuitional and cannot long be sustained, while the event narrated by Borges is an intellectual disillusionment reached by Tzinacán through reason, and it bears the earmarks of permanence. Each is a "mental process," but the former is emo-tionally and incidentally so, while the latter is self-conscious and philosophical, involving some kind of post-experiential decision. Both Valéry and Tzinacán come into a timelessness and a sort of universal vision; but Valéry achieves it by sensing the pulse of the universe, its form and rhythm, while Tzinacán does so by reflecting upon the self and its separation from truth. In the Symbolist ex-perience there is a restoration of life purpose, expressed in "The Marine Cemetery" as "One must try to live!" (*Il faut tenter de vivre!*). We sense that this is tantamount to a return to delusion, to action, and to hope. But Tzinacán is given the quiet comfort of absolute despair: "I let the days forget me, lying here in the darkness." The Symbolists evince doubt and optimism; Borges shows despair and will. They, despite their skepticism of language, are optimistic about truth; he is pessimistic, but positively so. He seems to share in the "positive pessimism" of Hans Vaihinger, whom I shall bring up farther on.

When the outer world is seen as illusion, thought is bereft of an object and can only turn inward upon itself. Roger Shattuck has shown how the poetry of the French avant-garde (1885 to World War I) is characterized by inwardness; it is an "art of stillness," of permeating circularity—a self-reflexive "art about art" (*The Banquet Years*, pp. 325–352). It seeks the pinnacle experience of Valéry, which is the intuitional counterpart of Borges' intellectual Aleph, and which is perhaps the same thing as Breton's "point":

Everything leads one to believe that there is a certain point of the spirit where life and death, the real and the imaginary, the past and the future, the communicable and the uncommunicable, the high and the low, cease to be perceived as contradictory. So in surrealist activity it is useless to look for any other motive than the hope of determining that point.[6]

The transcending of logical contradictions is of course the object and accomplishment of religion, to which Raymond says poetry long ago became supplementary (p. 5). Shattuck speaks of the feeling of modern poets that "God will come as an outgrowth or a construct of mind—man surpassing himself" (p. 42). But this is what Borges no longer believes; it is precisely here that he differs from Valéry and the other mystics of the avant-garde and the sundry "isms" that Ultraism aspired to outdo. Borges does not believe that man can surpass himself; he is no mystic. His art is not truth and does not seek truth. It does not transcend anything, but undercuts everything by driving downward and backward to the

[6] André Breton, *Manifestes du surréalisme*, pp. 76–77. The translation is mine.

ground of things—to the natural metaphysic, the point to which, Urban says, "the mind inevitably comes if it follows the 'natural bent of the intellect' to its conclusion" (p. 688).

It has been said and resaid that to Borges literature is only a game that men play; not as the Dadaists played it, with desperate frivolity, but somewhat as Mallarmé saw it: "a solemn, regulated, and significant game." To this, however, we must add the element of humor. Borges is funny, both as a writer and as a person, and he delights in being so. He is forever spoofing and poking fun. His conviction that all cerebration is but useful fictionmaking is the source of his ironic humor and is no doubt the basic reason for his split with Ultraism, for the Ultraists seriously wanted to supersede all of the "isms" that splintered from the trunk of art around the turn of the century—to get at the *ultra*, the beyond. Thus Ultraism continued the spirit that was born with Romanticism: the mystique that made art, as Raymond says again, "an ethic or some kind of irregular instrument of metaphysical knowledge" (p. 5). Borges stopped believing in that power of poetry; in his view neither reason nor art has an answer to man's senseless question about the meaning of the universe.

The difference between Borges and his doubting, hoping forerunners is the best confirmation of his truly intellectual esthetic. From another standpoint we could as easily group him with Valéry, Mallarmé, Rousseau, and others and call him a mystic in the broad sense. The tension which all of them would like to see dissolved is the one between the outer, unknown cosmos and whatever scheme the consciousness may hypostatize and dogmatize as truth; a tension between pantheism and monotheism, between universal vision and perspectivism, between Aleph and Zahir. James Irby calls this tension in Borges' work "the central dilemma of the contingent and the absolute."[7] The esthetic consciousness overcomes this tension by the simple expedient of having a skeptical, fluid, shifting point

[7] "The Structure of the Stories of Jorge Luis Borges," p. 289.

of view. It assigns only brief validity to the various perspectives of the universe, forming and dissolving them in sequence until, in memory at least, they are all present at once, building in an imperfect way the comprehensive Aleph. In concept the process is the same as that of piling up symbols around the vacancy where the unnamed reality is inferred or intuited. These "near moments" are almost always associated in Borges' stories with the images of vertigo, inebriation, exaltation, alcohol, delirium, fever, and perhaps happiness (*vértigo, embriaguez, exaltación, alcohol, delirio, fiebre, felicidad*). This is difficult to illustrate at this point in the study because it requires interpretation of symbols in context; perhaps a few brief examples of the uses of just one of them, dizziness, will be useful. In "The Secret Miracle" the protagonist Hladík dreams that he is in the Library of Clementinum looking for God, who is in one of the letters in one of the hundreds of thousands of books. The map containing the tiny letter is called vertiginous (*vertiginoso*), and the adjective is made to apply ambiguously to Hladík as well, for he is about to discover God: "He saw a map of India, vertiginous" (*F*, 164; *Lab.*, 92; *Fic.*, 148). There is another such case in "The House of Asterion" where the narrator says, "I run through the stone galleries until I roll to the ground, dizzy"; here the masculine adjective *mareado* can apply both to the narrator and to the ground, *suelo* (*A*, 68; *Lab.*, 139). The parable of the Simurg in "The Approach to Almotásim" (*F*, 42; *Fic.*, 43; told in more detail in *M*, 43) gives a mythological allegory on the protagonist's search for the ultimate: the birds go in search of their king, crossing seven valleys or seas; "the name of the penultimate is Vertigo; the last is called Annihilation." The gaucho Cruz ("Biography of Tadeo Isidoro Cruz") finds his true identity in a moment of dizziness; he is "dizzy from loss of blood" when he "hears his name" and "sees his face" (*A*, 55). The usurper Otálora (in "The Dead Man") comes near to achieving glory in a dizzy, drunken moment metaphorized as a "tower of vertigoes" (*A*, 33). In "The Shape of the Sword" the moment of truth is near when a traitor is being chased by a vengeful patriot through "black corridors of nightmare and deep stairways of vertigo" (*F*, 135; *Lab.*, 71; *Fic.*, 122). The man-dreaming magician of "The Circular Ruins" has difficulty in molding his creation out of "the incoherent and vertiginous material that dreams are made of" (*F*, 162; *Lab.*, 47; *Fic.*, 59). Let me add that here and there Borges seems to make an equation between "annihilation"—the post-esthetic delusion of truth (or truth-as-language)—and salvation, happiness, or even death. To have a truth is a form of "lucidity" or "insomnia" as opposed to sleeping or dreaming, which is creation or imagination. In the masterful story "The Lottery in Babylon," where Babylon is "a vertiginous country," the good fortunes of individuals who win in the lottery are alluded to as "happinesses" (*felicidades*). If we think of the citizens of Babylon as *mental* beings (attributes occasionally lifted to substantiality by the momentary attention of the consciousness), each "happiness" can be interpreted as a configuration of thought —a hypostatization, a conceptual reality. Borges says of them: "In many cases, the knowledge that certain felicities were mere fabrications of chance would have diminished their virtue" (*F*, 71; *Lab.*, 33; *Fic.*, 68).

In Borges' stories there are countless such dizzy, fevered, exalted moments when someone is about to see the truth (or thinks he is), when a man is close to self-understanding, when some half-entity is about to come into full being, when the ultimate is about to be revealed. At least one of the stories seems to have the "esthetic fact" as its whole motivation. "The End" is a fanciful addendum to the *Martín Fierro* of José Hernández. The setting is the Argentine pampa where the famed gaucho Fierro is about to fight to the death with a Negro enemy. The tension set up in this rivalry is esthetic; in the ambiguity of the dual existence of the abstraction "gaucho" (Fierro and the Negro are both gauchos) there is a suggestion of "gaucho" as a Platonic form. We can surmise that if one of the rivals dies, the other will remain as the sole embodiment or lone symbol of the form; the man will be lifted to the plane of the universal, or the universal will be rendered particular, as you will; in any case the tension and indefiniteness will be destroyed. The possibility, the pregnancy, will be spoiled by the form's incarnation in a single "word."

It is consistent with this esthetic ambiguity that the only on-looker at the fight, a storekeeper named Recabarren, suffers a stroke and becomes paralyzed and speechless—for the esthetic experience is unspeakable and the mythic or circular world view is characterized by stasis. (Paralysis is also one of the attributes of Ireneo Funes in "Funes the Memorious": his mind is so cluttered with lucid details that he cannot form abstractions). The gauchos fight on a vast plain that is "almost abstract, as if seen in a dream" (F, 178; Fic., 160). Almost abstract; that is, still indefinite and esthetically loaded, its Name not yet spoken. Indefinite, I repeat, not necessarily polyvalent. Again referring to the plain, Borges gives us a paraphrase of his definition of the "esthetic reality":

There is an hour of the afternoon when the plain [llanura, flatness] is about to say something; it never says it, or perhaps it says it infinitely and we do not understand it, or we understand it but it is untranslatable like a music . . . (F, 180; Fic., 162).

And when the Negro has killed Fierro, becoming synonymous with the Platonic form that had subsumed them both, he loses his individual identity and is universalized. Now he is nobody and everybody, including Fierro: "Now he was no one. Or rather, he was the other one" (F, 180; Fic., 162).

The something that the pampa was about to say was sacrificed in the moment of its imperfect embodiment in "language," or in the moment of its formulation as idea. Had both men stayed alive, the esthetic tension would have remained as a wordless "poem" or as a near-incarnation of truth; an avatar, perhaps in the form of a metaphor. But when Fierro died a name was spoken and the poem ended.

This interpretation of "The End" places the story very near, if not in, the category of allegory. The question whether his stories are allegorical seems to have plagued Borges. He has called that genre "an error," has discussed it much, has called at least one of his stories "alegoría" ("The Cult of the Phoenix," termed allegory in the prologue to *Artificios*; *F*, 116; *Fic.*, 105), and he seems to have felt the allegorical trend in most of his fictions. I would not argue this point; Borges' stories can have such a multiplicity of meanings that they are rightly called polyvalent and are perhaps therefore allegorical on a high level. But these tales also evince the quality of indefiniteness, just as the *hecho estético* is characterized by it; and vagueness, not polyvalence, is considered to be the hallmark of the true symbol (cf. William York Tindall, *The Literary Symbol*, p. 21). Borges' allegories, if they are that, are of so lofty a type that they comprise a unique kind of symbolism. His frequent evocation of the conceptual form of the esthetic phenomenon as he conceives it, wrought in a Symbolist manner through allusion and suggestion, is a rare thing: a symbolism of Symbolism. But I would not argue if the final verdict of critics maintains allegory, nothing more; it still comprises a way in which a Symbolist, or anyone else, can picture to himself the form of his own mental process. "Art," said Borges, "must show us our own face" (*H*, 101; *Dream.*, 89).

The esthetic experience is essentially intellectual, but it is not usually self-conscious; it does not analyze itself in the moment of its occurrence. But when, in literature, this happening consists precisely in its looking at itself through symbolic or allegorical forms, the reader is given a degree of control over the event. Because he has some awareness of what is happening, as it happens, he can surrender to the esthetic enjoyment, or he can concentrate on the manner of production of the esthetic occurrence with intellectual appreciation, or he can do both at once with the effect of unifying and heightening his experience. A person can read and reread Borges with the enjoyment he feels in replaying his favorite music.

The Symbolists made their poetry self-symbolizing, but perhaps took the matter too seriously. This is not to say that they damaged their poetry; but their seriousness affected adversely some of those who followed, creating a number of diverging and short-lived "isms." They looked for God through poetry; they tried to be mythic in order to restructure the universe. But Borges, both as poet and as fiction-maker, knows that modern man cannot be mythic, not really, and that imagination only confirms idealism as the nearest substitute for a mythic view; for in order to be mythic, the mind must lack a structured rationality. Only man's reason can call into question the hierarchy of reality it has created. The conceptual fluidity of the mythmaker can exist only as a mentality that radically doubts the validity of its own constructs, or as one which consciously forays into fancy without expecting to transcend or fulminate the vast system of practical fictions that men live by. Borges will not ride with Valéry on the seesaw of momentary subjective renewal followed by reentry into mundane reality; this smacks of psychedelic self-hypnosis, of religion, of escape. Borges will not lose psychic control over the game; he will remain the chess player as well as the pawn.

To put it differently, the Symbolists apparently believed they could break out of the conceptual cosmos through intuition—through perception without conception. Borges knows that this is an esthetic delusion and that conception is inevitable. Men are doomed to possess their world as language which cannot bespeak the objective order but can only reflect the imperfect memories of the mind. Experiences of the pregnant moments do not remain as full-blown images, but as mere language that stands where reality used to be. "When the end is near, the images of the remembrance do not remain; only words" ("The Immortal," A, 25; Lab., 118).

The Rending of the Veil

*J*N THE FOREGOING CHAPTER I have tried to place Borges in a proper literary context, because from here on I shall deal with him from a point of view that may appear limited and almost extra-literary. But it is a viewpoint that implies much more than is encompassed in the words that express it. If I seem to treat Borges' short stories as if they were primarily the artistic reflection of a few ancient ideas about the functions of the mind, it is because I must be simplistic for the sake of putting this one aspect of his work into clear relief. It is one of the most important aspects of his fictional creation.

This is an expediency which Borges himself—author of "The Zahir" and "The Aleph"—would not despise. When Carlos Argentino Daneri takes Borges into his cellar to show him the magic Aleph (a point in space where the universe can be seen at a glance), Borges is told that he must lie flat on the floor and hold his head at a certain angle. I suggest to the reader of this book that the same concession will be necessary if he is to see what I hope to show: that there is system in Borges, a method in his fantasy. This is to say that the reader must bear with me as I lay out some rather technical ideas about human thought and a bit of terminology which will be indispensable to the study. Some of this will be a paraphrase of the central idea of the first chapter. I must point out that in dealing with a few concepts about the human mind, I do not purport to be in harmony with systematic philosophy or psychology. Neither, in fact, is Borges; he has read much philosophy, but he has read eclectically and has eloped with his favorite ideas, loving them as an artist and not as a systematic thinker. I have done much the same, particularly in abstracting some pertinent ideas from Vaihinger.

Borges' intellectual esthetic, his "imminence of a revelation," his "mental process," and his penchant for the depiction of ambiguity, are facets of the self-expression of a mind inverted upon itself. Borges wrote:

A man sets himself the task of outlining the world. Through the years he peoples a space with images of provinces, kingdoms, mountains, bays, ships, islands, fishes, dwellings, instruments, stars, horses, and persons. A little before he dies, he discovers that that patient labyrinth of lines traces the image of his face (*H*, 109; *Dream.*, 93).

What, then, is the essential nature, the identity, of the mountains and horses and persons with whom Borges peoples his literature, if in the end they trace the image of Borges, who knows them for what they are? They are ideal beings, the constructions of a self-conscious mind, and we can expect them to behave as such, not as the mountains and horses and persons that we know in the outer world. Borges' labyrinths can disappear when confronted with words that equate to them; Averroes vanishes on looking into a mirror; two men are one man; men gain and lose immortality; they are called omnipotent while they move about impotently; and they see the universe under a stair, or the universe is hidden from them behind a coin. The dissolution of the rational order in Borges' fiction brings forcefully to mind the characteristics of mythical thinking as they are enumerated by Mircea Eliade, Ernst Cassirer, Sir James Frazer, and other writers on the subject of prelogical thought. Some of these traits or ideas are: circular or static time; sacred and meaningless time; the oneness of all being (monism); the equation of a part of anything with the whole of it; the equality of language and reality; the fluidity of the human personality, the solubility of the "I," and the obliteration of the distinction between life and death; cosmic predestination and the impotence of man; the dissolution of space and time, and their inseparability from their specific content; indistinct and sacred numbers; and *hypostatization*—the making of "gods." The world in which Borges' fictive creations move about is a primeval world and has all the earmarks of the archaic cosmology.

This is owing precisely to the fundamental fluidity of Borges' thought. Borges is an idealist, a skeptic, a freethinker, and above all, an artist. The human mind imagines and conjectures in the same degree that it does not know, or in the degree to which it does not choose to know or does not believe it knows. Radical speculation—imagination—is the special property of archaic man, who has little fixed knowledge to guide him; of children for the same reason; and of the artist, the poet, and the skeptic. Where facts have not yet been chosen or have been rejected for scientific or esthetic reasons, fantasies compete for honor. Every truth begins as metaphor, useful fiction, or esthetic dream. As I shall show later on, Borges allegorizes this situation as a college of imaginary students competing for the privilege of becoming real.

Men have always felt that their thoughts were only dreams, and their language, philosophy, science, and literature have testified to this from the beginning. To think is to abstract, and to abstract is to "draw out," to select one facet of reality and lift it above all others and call it the essence or the whole truth. The name given to the whole conjunct of attributes really denotes only the aggrandized part, merely connoting the other qualities or forgetting them completely. In order to speak of Borges' imagery and symbol without undue verbiage, I must adopt a word, *hypostat*, to signify this enlarged facet which, in the act of thinking, is hypostatized—called a substantial thing—while the other attributes remain adjectival appendages. Farther on I will try to show that Borges characterizes this mental process of forming, dissolving, and re-forming mental conjuncts as the Lottery in Babylon, with the momentary winners being mental hypostatizations and the losers, or connotations, being depicted as citizens who are fined, punished, or jailed.

I have already mentioned that Urban's *philosophia perennis* depends on a substance-attribute concept of being. Philosophers as early as Plato spoke in the same terms, and among the more recent thinkers who accorded honor to thing and attribute was Vaihinger, who made it important in his philosophy of fictions.[1] When seen from the standpoint of thing-attribute, every human idea may be said to look like a little pyramid, with the essential feature of reality sitting atop the minor characteristics and dominating them; or it is like a hero being carried on the shoulders of a crowd; or it is like an upright structure—a tower, a pole, an obelisk—standing on a flat surface. The psychologists would probably let these images pass as metaphorical representations of a Gestalt. Epistemologists would perhaps accept them from a layman as depictions of one of the first principles of thought, *pars pro toto*, or simply as representations of perspectivizing. Writers of a mythical or symbolistic bent seem to accept the avoidance of this kind of abstraction as the central dilemma of creation in our time: how to create the uncrowned pyramid, the incomplete or pregnant Gestalt,

[1] Hans Vaihinger, *The Philosophy of 'As If,'* pp. 164–172.

the mythic situation just prior to the incarnation of the god, the poetic ambiguity that is *almost abstract*. Without this creation there can be no truly mythic quality in literature, no polyvalence, no true symbolism as we now understand it.

Carried to a higher plane, the form of an idea becomes the form of a whole hierarchy of knowledge. A system, said Borges, is the subordination of all aspects of the universe to any one of them (*F*, 23; *Lab.*, 10; *Fic.*, 25). The process of mentally dissolving and remaking the world (imagination, conjecture, fantasy) is a matter of demoting the dominant characteristics of things and raising other qualities in their place. Poets and writers do this all the time; in rhetoric, metonymy is a device for relating objects to each other through qualities held in common which are momentarily treated as essential but which are not essences when judged from a conventional standpoint.[2] Rationality is a synonym for the prosaic.

The implications of this simple procedure of idea-reformation are profound. When the consciousness impeaches a dominant feature of reality, a hypostat, it negates the history of thought and returns momentarily to the primordial chaos—to the world of sense perception without *conception*, to an awareness that is prior to idea; that is, it goes back to the uncreated, the amorphous, the farthest point from "truth." It does this very briefly before abstracting another quality to replace the one degraded, so that in all imagination there is a suggestion of the indistinct, the mythic, the esthetic. Since the word *myth* does not belong to any branch of learning in particular and has a dozen meanings, let us follow Langer and adopt it here to signify this pregnant, primeval condi-

---

[2] James E. Irby ("The Structure of the Stories of Jorge Luis Borges," pp. 121, 143–144) has pointed out that metonymy is an important device in Borges' world-dissolution. Adolfo Bioy Casares, Borges' friend and collaborator, may be speaking of the same kind of fantasy in the Prologue to his and Borges' anthology of fantastic literature (*Antología de la literatura fantástica*, p. 13), when he observes that the "obsessions" in Kafka's work constitute "hierarchical subordination."

tion in which all the attributes of being are set out in a democratic
line like soldiers standing at parade prior to the selection of any
one of them to be captain over the others. I use the word without
the article to avoid confusion with the conventional idea of "a
myth," which can only imply a hypostat because a myth is a
mental configuration, an idea. The formation of an idea destroys
myth; human thought is inimical to myth because logical, objective, discursive thought is abstraction.

Lest I seem inconsistent, let me point out that the sacredness or
pregnancy which Langer imputes to myths or mythic beliefs is in
fact owing to what these imply as egregious or magic truths. The
simultaneous existence of contradictory ideas, or the existence of
a truth that is alien to the main body of knowledge, is compelling
because it implies a transcending realm in which contradictions are
resolved and magic is not magic. Every myth insinuates a whole
ontology.

But myth, as I am using the term, is not to be conceived as a
ground existing only beneath the lowest level of abstraction. On
the contrary, it exists on any plane where an abstraction seems
possible but is not yet made. Perhaps I am only talking about one
kind of symbolism, the "indefiniteness" of Tindall; if so, critics
have failed to ascribe to indefiniteness the fundamental importance
that it seems to have in literary history and oral tradition.

When the mind becomes profoundly aware that abstraction is
a distortion of reality, it becomes skeptical, idealist. It is no longer
capable of regarding any of its hypostatizations as objectively true.
It sees thought as something to be engaged in provisionally, as
conscious fictionalizing, but it does not deny the utility and
necessity of it. Above the empirical world, however, there is no
criterion of truth or utility, and thinking can be proven or justified
only by the need of the consciousness to preserve its integrity and
peace. The esthetic criterion is likely to be substituted for all
others. In so far as "esthetic" means "ambiguous," the skeptical
intellect becomes reinforced in its opposition to dogma. It delights

in the panoramic and the kaleidoscopic, because these imply that an underlying or transcending viewpoint is possible. That is, the very fluidity, the change of perspectives, is esthetic because it implies something beyond.

Someone once said that the Germans are always making myths (here we mean hypostats) and that the French are always denying them. This testifies to a fundamental difference of cultures which has been pointed out many times over; the Germanic peoples tend to create monolithic ideas or structures of mind, conducive to a certain dynamism, while the Latin peoples are more philosophical or analytical and try always to keep all the facets of a situation in view. So we call the Latin cultures esthetic and relatively static, and the Saxon cultures are said to be dynamic, utilitarian, and materialistic. However valid this idea may be, it points to the same thing that Isaiah Berlin, the British historian, has noted as a psychic difference in the mentalities of many great writers. He makes his point by quoting Archilochus: "The fox knows many things, but the hedgehog knows one big thing" (*The Hedgehog and the Fox*, p. 7). Shakespeare, Goethe, and Aristotle are foxes in this scheme; Dante, Plato, and Dostoevsky are hedgehogs. Perhaps the distinction is merely that of Nominalism versus Realism, Aristotle against Plato. According to Berlin, Tolstoy was a crossbreed; he "was by nature a fox, but believed in being a hedgehog" (p. 11). How would Borges fit into the scheme?

I would say that Borges is philosophically a fox who longs for the simplicity and certainty of the hedgehog but cannot bring himself to be one. He searches, without hope of finding, something which transcends fox and hedgehog. He finds only substitutes and metaphors for that transcending something. Intellectually, he finds idealism; esthetically, myth. Borges is both an Anglophile and an Argentine. He is steeped in the mood of Schopenhauer and Nietzsche and in English literature, but emotionally he is a product of Spanish American *criollismo*. He has made the conflict between perspectivism and universal vision (Zahir and Aleph) one of his central artistic concerns (I would maintain that it is *the* central concern), and he depicts the transcendence of this contradiction as myth, the near-abstraction or esthetic fact. Because of this central concern, Borges is literarily a hedgehog.

This is the most important point to be made in this study of Borges' fiction. The system that is apparent in Borges' imagery and symbol hinges upon the simple idea of pyramidal thought, of thing and attribute, with all of its vast implications. I shall try to show that when Borges speaks of twilight and noon, swamps and towers, blood and sand, tigers and walls, and dozens of other things that recur in his fiction, he is talking about being and non-being, the created and the uncreated; and always he is talking about them with the implication that the contradiction between them is transcended—or as I see it, underlain—by myth. Myth is the place where Valéry goes when he goes out of time. It is the moment between the death of an idea and the birth of another—when, as in the case of Tzinacán, the universe is glimpsed, when the soul is aware without knowing what it is aware of, hearing the wordless poem of Mallarmé. Such moments bring the feeling of omnipotence, for the mind senses that it can make of reality whatever it wishes; there is an illusion of clairvoyance, because all the details of the world are equally available or remote. This is a common psychic happening, and only the poets and the mystics seem able to prolong it; they stretch it out by declaring that the world and all of its details are somehow provisional and illusory. The idealist prolongs or converts the "moment" into an intellectual attitude. We call it pantheism, nihilism, skepticism, or intellectual mysticism, but Borges is nearest to right in calling it an esthetic of the intelligence.

With terrible irony, fate has made Borges almost blind, as if in token of his intellectual agnosticism. Hans Vaihinger, also an idealist and author of a philosophy of illusions, suffered the same progressive weakness of the eyes leading to blindness. Reading Vaihinger's *Philosophy of 'As If,'* one can hardly keep from suppos-

ing a direct influence on Borges' "Tlön, Uqbar, Orbis Tertius,"
particularly since the *Philosophie des Als Ob* is mentioned in the
story (*F*, 13; *Lab.*, 10; *Fic.*, 25; Vaihinger's works are also alluded
to in *M*, 20). But Borges told a critic in 1967 that he had never read
Vaihinger.[3] I do not make a case, therefore, for any influence of
Vaihinger upon Borges; but some of the philosopher's ideas, taken
at random, are so useful in speaking of Borges' idealism and his
esthetic, and the attitudes of the two men are so similar, that I
cannot resist using one to place the other in bolder outline. One of
the objectives of Vaihinger's philosophy is to liberate men, he says,
from the sublime-catastrophic nature of dogmatism, the illusion of
having truth. It argues, so to speak, for the right of Borges to create
his own world and affirms the practical necessity of his doing it.
The system justifies idealism of an ethico-esthetic type: the self-
enclosure of the intellect and the building of a conceptual cosmos
complete in itself and at peace with itself. The philosophy is an
oxymoron—a positive pessimism or "idealist positivism"—a way of
saying that the good is not to be identified with the objectively
true but with the subjectively true; the world can be known only
as it is practically symbolized to the mind by the mind itself in the
realization that the world and the mind are not separate things:
one is a part of the other.

Borges is preoccupied with creation in any sense of that word.
He points to it in most of his stories, but nowhere more completely
than in a story already mentioned, "The Writing of the God," in
which the prisoner Tzinacán builds a lofty tower of illusions during
his years of trying to decipher the meaning of the world. This
hidden meaning is contained in the writing of a god on the skin of
a tiger. Tzinacán's ideas and thoughts are "dreams within dreams,"
he is told, and he will die before he can "unwalk" the "interminable
road"—that is, before he can think his way back to the mythical
flatness prior to thought-distortion where the universe can be seen

[3] See Jean de Milleret, *Entretiens avec Jorge Luis Borges*, p. 157.

as it really is. Immediately abandoning the illusion of knowledge, he "sees the universe" as a circle, all things in it as unsubsumed and original details, and himself as one of them. He experiences the complete loss of desire or will (the cause of his delusions) and understands the writing of the god.

But in Borges the uses of this fallacy, thought, are as important as its failures. Since man's ideas cannot be validated by outside criteria, one idea is as good as another. A man can demolish and reconstruct the world, making it less banal and more beautiful, and he can do this with the complete freedom of the self-sufficient mind. With regard to this idealist solipsism, Anderson Imbert says that what interests Borges is the beauty of the theories, myths, and beliefs that he cannot believe in; he feels free to choose "a multiplicity of simultaneous paths" (*Literatura hispanoamericana,* II, 268). As this critic goes on to say, Borges sees man as lost in a labyrinth, capable of producing mental labyrinths of his own as explanations of the chaotic Great Labyrinth. But while men in general engage in serious hypostatization as the only form of "explanation," Borges stands above this attempt to account for the universe; his truth does not depend on the things that can be called true, but upon the assumption that nothing can be so called. For him the goal of thought is not knowledge, but distraction.

Borges' most lucid symbol of this mental isolation from objective reality is the Minotaur of "The House of Asterion." This story can be read coherently and meaningfully if one keeps in mind that the narrator, Asterion, is the idealist consciousness and that the labyrinth he lives in is the conceptual universe:

I know they accuse me of pride, and perhaps of misanthropy, and perhaps of madness. . . . It is true that I do not leave my house, but it is also true that its doors . . . are open. . . . Let whoever will come in. . . . [Here there is] quiet and solitude. . . . Even my detractors admit that there is not *one piece of furniture* in the house. Another ridiculous idea is that I, Asterion, am a prisoner. . . . I cannot lose myself in the mob, although my modesty might desire it. . . . The fact is that I am unique.

I am not interested in what one man may transmit to other men; like the philosopher, I think that nothing is communicable through the art of writing. Annoying and trivial details have no place in my spirit, which is made for all that is grand (*A*, 67–68; *Lab.*, 138–139).

Speaking as Asterion, Borges describes how he can soar to heights of esthetic enjoyment, but only as a diversion whose end is impotence:

Naturally I do not lack distractions. Like a ram about to charge, I run through the galleries of stone until I roll to the ground, dizzy. . . . There are roofs from which I let myself fall until I bloody myself (*A*, 68; *Lab.*, 139).

He describes the mind's examination of its own nature, its effort to hold a self-defining dialogue with its projected image (or with other minds), looking at the conceptual universe in various perspectives:

But of all these games the one I prefer is the one about another Asterion. I pretend that he comes to visit me and that I show him the house. With great obeisances I say to him: *Now we go back to the former intersection* or *Now we are coming out into another patio* . . . or *Now you will see a cistern that filled up with sand* . . . (*A*, 68; *Lab.*, 139).

Here the mind examines its conceptual structure of the world:

Not only have I imagined these games, but I have also meditated upon the house. All the parts of the house are present many times; any place is another place. . . . The house is the size of the world; or rather, it is the world (*A*, 68; *Lab.*, 139).

But finally, and pathetically, Borges confesses the longing of the self-enclosed intellect for deliverance from its endless, meaningless conjecturing; death, or knowledge, is a redeemer who can deliver man from the confusing complexity of consciousness:

. . . because I know that my redeemer lives and in the end will rise above the dust. . . . I hope he will take me to a place with fewer galleries and fewer doors (*A*, 69–70; *Lab.*, 140).

When Asterion's redeemer comes, in the form of his executioner, Theseus, the poor creature hardly defends himself.

I will come back to this story. For the moment let it be kept in mind that among the images mentioned prominently are stone, dust, blood, dizziness, sand, and the bronze sword of Theseus. In particular, the house of Asterion is of stone, like the circular cell of Tzinacán, and the Minotaur's redeemer will "rise above the dust."

Each of Borges' stories, generally speaking, gives only one or another aspect of the overall form of conceptualizing, the most complete representation being made, perhaps, in "Tlön, Uqbar, Orbis Tertius." In at least two other stories we can see clearly how Borges plays both sides of the same record: he depicts hypostatization itself and then its opposite. In "The Zahir" the narrator, Borges himself, is obsessed with a hypostat from which he cannot divert his attention, and in "Funes the Memorious" he displays the opposite affliction. Funes is unable to hypostatize anything, "almost incapable of general, Platonic ideas" (F, 125; Lab., 65; Fic., 114). He cannot forget irrelevancies while noticing essentials. "To think is to forget differences, to generalize, to abstract. In the cluttered world of Funes there were only details" (F, 126; Lab., 66; Fic., 115). Borges characterizes Funes' mental world, apparently, as that of primordial chaos before the human consciousness entered into linear time and into prophetic perspectivizing: "Ireneo was nineteen years old; he was born in 1868; to me he looked monumental like bronze, older than Egypt, anterior to the prophecies and the pyramids" (F, 127; Lab., 66; Fic., 115). Each of these extremes—the obsession with the Zahir and the inability of Funes to abstract—is an incapacity for dissolving or reconstructing the world, and this is a fatal ineptitude. Funes, full of details, dies of pulmonary congestion.

Taking fictional constructs as objective truths is, for Borges, the same thing as arriving at "salvation" or intellectual death. To find truth is to tear aside the veil that hides ultimate reality. In "The

Zahir" the object which bears that name is said to be "the shadow of the rose and the rending of the veil" (*A,* 112; *Lab.,* 163). In Babylon there are veiled men who utter blasphemous conjectures in the twilight (*F,* 68; *Lab.,* 31; *Fic.,* 66), and the truth-seeking student of "The Approach to Almotásim" finds the Ultimate just behind a curtain. Two outstanding works of literature are conspicuous for their use of the rose and the veil as symbols; one is the *Divine Comedy* of Dante, prominently suggested and satirized in "The Aleph," and the other is *The Rubáiyát of Omar Khayyám,* which could be called the virtual inspiration of "The Zahir."

Borges' penchant for remaking the world could not be more fittingly paraphrased than it is in this verse from Omar:

> Ah Love! Could you and I with Him conspire
> To grasp this sorry Scheme of Things entire,
>   Would not we shatter it to bits—and then
> Re-mold it nearer to the Heart's Desire![4] (xcix)

As a matter of fact, an approach to Borges' whole view of reality and of life, as it is manifest in his prose fiction and his essays, could not be better made than by placing the philosophy of Vaihinger alongside the Rubáiyát. I say this, keeping in mind the positivism of Vaihinger and at the same time the melancholy despair of Omar, which is overcome in the poem by hedonistic recourse to real or symbolic inebriation. This will be made clearer in the coming pages. First I must make a partial analysis of three of Borges' short stories and show their interrelationship and their connection with Omar.

Critics have applied the term "agnostic" to Borges, usually indirectly. Anderson Imbert speaks of his "agnostic vision" and Rafael Gutiérrez Girardot (*Jorge Luis Borges: ensayo de interpretación*) applies the epithet as a question, pointing out that Borges' distrust of any particular religion or metaphysical system is the

---

[4] This and subsequent quotations from *The Rubáiyát of Omar Khayyám* are taken from Edward FitzGerald's Fifth Translation.

corollary and foundation of his attitude toward poetry (p. 68). Marcial Tamayo and Adolfo Ruiz-Díaz (*Borges, enigma y clave*) see his metaphysics and his grammar as much the same thing, like Aristotle's:

... in Borges' work there is not the least hiatus between concretely verbal, grammatical questions and the steepest speculations of metaphysics (p. 14).

Borges recognizes that there are two basic approaches to the problem of conscious existence: to think or not to think. Thought is synonymous with imagination, for both consist in making fictions and they have the same form. To have an adequate fiction is to have "knowledge," and thought occurs only where knowledge is absent. The mere use and reuse of fixed categories—familiar Gestalten—is not thought, but automatism: ritual. The religion of the unquestioning believer and the unthinking activism of the materialist are (in this scheme of things) forms of automatism. In the stories to be examined below, they are characterized as the state of lucidity or wakefulness as opposed to thought (imagination), which is "dream." Automatism is the state of being present to the physical world; it does not raise metaphysical questions. One gets the feeling that for Borges the "lucid" automaton is not yet alive and that the person who truly achieves a vision of the universe (or an adequate substitute) has died. Life consists in illusion, *i.e.*, creation; and knowledge is, as Schiller said, death.

Intellectual death is both tempting and repugnant to Borges. He feels the tension between the insecurity of consciousness and the nonexistence of obliviousness. At this point the contradiction which religion and metaphysics attempt to overcome is evident: freedom versus predestination. How does Borges overcome it? He predicates final predestination, the negation of responsibility which alone can liberate the consciousness; for action is impossible and the mind cannot function where anything eternal depends on the outcome of its activity. Its function is creation, which requires freedom and presupposes the absence of "truth." The hell of the Buddhist is continued consciousness, and he seeks in his successive lives to achieve final annihilation. The problem of Borges lies in the tension between the freedom to live and make fictions (which are only fictions) and the temptation to become oblivious; deluded consciousness or secure death; freedom or certainty; self or no-self; being or nonbeing.

In this situation Borges chooses life, conjecture, freedom; but he can do it only by making the entire universe *not* a great Gestalt dominated by a hypostatized God, but a great "mythic situation" that is pregnant with unformulated idea. Thus all fixations, all truth, all rigid interpretations are evil, for they destroy vital conjecture in the name of truths that are so small they can fit in the human mind. For Borges, God must remain indefinite, conjectural, polyvalent—otherwise he is valueless because he too is an illusion. There must be a mind bigger than man's; there must be order beyond the disorder of the Library of Babel, a reason beyond mere rationality. This is agnosticism in the etymological sense of the word, but it is not unfaith. Borges transcends freedom (responsibility) and destiny by having both. God is dreaming Borges, and whatever Borges may dream, in his freedom, is but a part of that larger dream.

But Asterion is not free of the longing for certainty. Critics are currently giving attention to the roles of the women who appear at the beginning of Borges' two most pivotal stories: "The Aleph" and "The Zahir." Dante had his Beatrice as the symbol of his unattainable esthetic ideal, and Petrarch his Laura. Borges places his Beatriz Viterbo at the beginning of "The Aleph," and "The Zahir" begins with a postmortem description of the personality of Teodelina Villar. Both these women are dead, not so much because it makes them unattainable like Dante's Beatrice as because they represent the possibility of death itself—intellectual cessation. Both of them represent the form of thinking: continual perspectivizing. But Teodelina does this under the shadow of a hypostat—

a background value (in this case, the vicissitudes of fashion). Beatriz represents the same activity, but without any such over-shadowing hypostatization. Thus they are the same woman, the same mental process, but Teodelina is a thoughtless automaton, always present to the visible world, which she measures by the dictates of her fixation. She corresponds to the Zahir.

Beatriz is the best-loved of the two because she is more like Borges, presumably; the picture he gives of her is more like the form of his own esthetic or his world view. We see her only as a series of photographs—perspectives of her single personality—and our total image of her has the illusory form of the Aleph, that magic orb in which the universe is seen in all perspectives at once. It is the Beatriz of the photographs whom Borges adores—the many perspectives unsummarized, pregnant with suggestion. The Beatriz who appears later in the magic Aleph is the summarized Beatriz, a mummified corpse who in real life had written obscene letters. Borges finally judges the Aleph to be a falsity, but while standing before the photographs—the pretty poses, none of which was anything but a momentary image, a fiction—he murmurs adoringly, "Beatriz . . . beloved Beatriz . . . lost forever . . . it is I, I am Borges" (A, 162; Per., 148).

In speaking of Teodelina, Borges again uses the image of the photographs and suggests that they, taken as a whole, create an esthetic ideal; pictures of Teodelina adorned all the magazine covers around 1930, and this "plethora perhaps contributed to their judging her very beautiful" (A, 103; Lab., 156). In what he says of Teodelina we can see both the form of human thinking and the limitation or automatism caused by the presence of a background "truth":

Teodelina concerned herself less with beauty than with perfection. . . . She sought . . . irreproachable correctness in every act, but . . . the norms of her credo were not eternal; they bowed to the caprices of Paris and Hollywood. Teodelina Villar showed herself in orthodox places at the orthodox hour, with orthodox attributes, with orthodox disdain, but the disdain, the attributes, the hour and the places grew stale almost immediately and would serve (in the mouth of Teodelina Villar) as a definition of the banal. . . . She attempted continual metamorphoses, as if to flee from herself; the color of her hair and the forms of her coiffure were famously unstable. Her smile, her complexion, the slant of her eyes also changed. . . . The war gave her much to think about. With Paris occupied by the Germans, how could one follow the fashions? (A, 103–104; *Lab.*, 157).

Teodelina aged and gave up her career as a model and had to go and live in a more modest section of town. After her death, Borges visits the home of Teodelina and views her body. The description of the girl's appearance is that of a petrified hypostatization or a mind characterized by one:

. . . her features recovered the authority given by pride, money, youth, the consciousness of crowning a hierarchy, lack of imagination, limitations, stolidity. . . . I left her rigid among the flowers . . . (A, 105; *Lab.*, 158).

This stolid, limited, unimaginative crown of a hierarchy is a fixed, dead truth, and Borges leaves it among the flowers. Like Tennyson's flower, which implies the universe as a hierarchy of being, these flowers are symbols of conventional hypostatization. Teodelina was "less concerned with beauty"—that is, with esthetic ambiguity—than with "perfection," with completed and unambiguous forms.

The dead woman of "The Aleph" is Beatriz Viterbo, cousin of Carlos Argentino Daneri; the latter name suggests Dante Alighieri. Borges' description of her is but the naming of her photographs on a wall in her brother's house:

Beatriz Viterbo, in profile and in color; Beatriz, with mask, at carnival in 1921; Beatriz' first communion; Beatriz, shortly after her divorce, at a luncheon in the Riding Club; Beatriz in Quilmes with Delia San Marco Porcel and Carlos Argentino; Beatriz with the Pekingese that Villegas Haedo gave her; Beatriz, from the front and at an angle, smiling, with her hand on her chin . . . (A, 151–152; *Per.*, 139).

As I said, Borges adores Beatriz as a series of photographs—flat, two-dimensional images of an ideal. If she were present as a flesh-and-blood reality she would be like the Aleph, all perspectives at once in three dimensions; she would be false by virtue of being too true. In life she was one of those women that a man can both love and hate. Only in his mind can Borges have the lovely Beatriz; Dante did not want Beatrice in the flesh. Having Beatriz would be tantamount to having truth, being dead, seeing the universe—but only a small universe, smaller than the mind.

Both in art and in fact, Beatriz is related to her cousin Carlos Argentino Daneri. He has written an endless poem in cantos (like Dante) in which he catalogues the entire universe as he has seen it in the Aleph. His poem is like the mind of Funes, endless detail and no conclusions, no creations. In Daneri's poetry Borges has been said to be satirizing his own. I don't quite agree; but if he is, he is making a parody on more than his literature, both here and in other writings where he is supposedly self-critical. He satirizes himself as a man, an imaginative organism who can do no more than imagine the world. The Aleph is finally the symbol of Borges himself—the symbol of any self-complete intelligence or self-coherent system of thought. Borges, the Aleph, the many philosophies and religions—they are all finally false. The Zahir is false, Funes is false. Myth itself, which is the flat and fallow ground without falsifying hypostatizations, is false too—because it is conceivable. Anything that can be thought is, to Borges, an illusion or conjecture, and anything which purports to be more than that becomes a lie because it gives rigidity and finality—smallness and finitude—to the universe and equates man with God.

I have pointed out that the obsession with the Zahir is a prototype of the inability to break up and reorganize reality, and that Funes has the opposite maladjustment, an incapacity to form abstractions. The Aleph and the Zahir represent the two conceivable forms of understanding: the transcending vision and the meaningful perspective; Funes represents the conceptual duplication of the universe down to the last detail. Borges sees all three of these avenues to reality as illusions. The three stories in which they are presented have various features and details in common: the repetition of images and words, parallel ideas and structures, a cryptic mention of oxymoron in connection with both of the women, and so on. Using one of his most frequent symbols of hypostatization—money or coin—Borges appropriately relates idealist fluidity (provisional hypostatizing) with dynamic, linear time as opposed to the fixed, circular time of traditional and archaic man:

Money is abstract, I repeated, money is future time. . . . It is unforeseeable time, Bergson time, not the hard time of Islam or of the Portico. . . . A coin symbolizes our free will (*A*, 107; *Lab.*, 159).

But an obsession gives the illusion of free will while in fact it denies it; nothing could remove the Zahir from Borges: ". . . I was unable to change my fixed idea" (*A*, 109; *Lab.*, 161). Beatriz is precisely that form of idealist fluidity that Borges adores; she plays with successive Zahires as a child plays with dolls, and is like a child:

Beatriz (I myself usually say it) was a woman, a child, of an almost implacable clear-sightedness, but in her there were negligences, distractions, disdains, real cruelties (*A*, 162; *Per.*, 147).

Her cousin Carlos Argentino is childlike too: "The child was, as always, in the cellar developing photographs" (*A*, 162; *Per.*, 148).

The act of beholding the entire universe is like the experience of the mystics, Borges says, but it can be expressed only in the forms of the Zahir, as successive snapshots or perspectives, each of which may imply the others in some measure:

All language is an alphabet of symbols whose use presupposes a past shared by all the users. How shall I transmit to others the infinite Aleph . . . ? The mystics, in analogous crisis, multiply emblems prodigally: to signify the divinity, a Persian speaks of a bird which is somehow all birds; Alanus of Insulis of a sphere whose center is everywhere and whose circumference is nowhere; Ezekiel of an angel with four faces who at one time looks to the east and west, north and south. . . . The central problem is unresolvable: the enumeration, even partial, of an infinite conjunct. . . . What my eyes saw was simultaneous; what I shall transcribe, successive, because language is successive (*A*, 163–164).

The Aleph and the Zahir are finally twin falsities, two aspects of the same daydream; the *a priori* and the *a posteriori* approaches to the unapproachable:

Tennyson said that if we could understand a single flower we would know who we are and what the world is. Perhaps he meant to say that there is no fact, however humble, that does not imply universal history and its infinite concatenation of causes and effects. Perhaps he meant to say that the visible world is fully present in every phenomenon, just as the will, according to Schopenhauer, is fully present in every individual. The Cabalists believed that man is a microcosm, a symbolic mirror of the universe; everything, according to Tennyson, would be. Everything, even the intolerable Zahir (*A*, 113; *Lab.*, 163).

"Zahir," Borges informs us, is Arabic for "visible" or "notorious." We note that Aleph is the first letter of the Hebrew alphabet (Arabic *alif*, Greek *alpha*); it begins with *A*, and Zahir with Z. We find an allusion to the *alif* in the fiftieth quatrain of the Rubáiyát:

> A Hair perhaps divides the False and True;
> Yes; and a single Alif were the clue—
> Could you but find it—to the Treasure-house
> And peradventure to the Master too.

Too little critical attention has been given to the connections between Borges' fiction and the FitzGerald translations of the Rubáiyát. Not only are there numerous correspondences of idea and imagery, but the very spirit of the Persian's poem is so like the world view evinced by Borges' works that if we adopted the mythic method of Borges himself we could make the two men momentarily and repeatedly identical. There is hardly a basic metaphysical idea in Borges that is not contained or implied in Omar. This is not to say that Borges has been in any way *caused* by FitzGerald.[5]

[5] Ana María Barrenechea (among others) refers to Borges' thematic use, in his "The Enigma of Edward FitzGerald" (*OI*, 109–114; *Oth. Inq.*, 75–78),

The Aleph and the Zahir have certain physical and functional similarities. Both are small, round objects; one gives a miraculous vision of the universe and the other blots out everything but itself, substituting for the universe. Both represent an escape from the world or a transformation of reality and the creation of the illusion of comprehension. Both are superficially desirable; even the "intolerable Zahir" does not cause suffering: "This would be tantamount to saying that the pain of an anesthetized man whose cranium is being opened is terrible" (A, 113; Lab., 164). The Aleph is a small sphere only two or three centimeters in diameter, and the Zahir is a small coin. Would it appear absurd to point out that the Aleph and the Zahir are about the size of the Grape that is extolled throughout the Rubáiyát?

> The Grape that can with logic absolute
> The Two-and-Seventy jarring sects confute:
>   The sovereign Alchemist that in a trice
> Life's leaden metal into gold transmute. (LIX)

Even the function is the same: world-dissolution and the creation of something new and shining. In "The Aleph" there is a coin image which also vaguely suggests alchemy: an allusion to persons "who do not have at their disposal precious metals nor steam presses, rolling mills and sulphuric acids for the coining of treasures, but who can *indicate* to *others* the location of a treasure" (A, 158; Per., 144). This allusion takes us back to the Treasure-house of Omar, and "The Zahir" also contains a mention of treasure: *un tesoro infinito* (A, 108; Lab., 160).

Both stories contain references to black and white tiles or flagstones, which we may take as Omar's "Checkerboard of Nights and Days" where men are played by Destiny as if they were pawns. In "The Zahir" there is an interior parable about the gold rings of the Niebelungs; in "The Aleph" there is an allusion to the "séptuple

---

of FitzGerald and Omar as personalities (*Expresión*, pp. 70–71; *Labyrinth Maker*, p. 16). She does not inquire into further relationships.

copa de Kai Josrú," which is the "Jamshyd's Sev'n-ring'd Cup" of the poem, deliberately misattributed to Omar's Kaikhosrú.

Before going into the *sótano* (*wine* cellar, probably) to see the Aleph, Borges is given a glass of wine by Carlos, who calls it "the pseudo cognac," no doubt because the real wine is the Aleph itself, the Grape. In all of Khayyám's poem, there are three primary symbols: the grape, the rose, and the veil. The Zahir is "the shadow of the rose and the rending of the veil"; whoever sees the Zahir will soon see the rose (*A*, 112; *Lab.*, 163), for the veil is rent apart.[6] The whole of "The Zahir" has an Islamic backdrop, and this gives occasion for Borges to place many small items from the Rubáiyát into the story; he has to insert them arbitrarily into "The Aleph," and does so, including a hint at the name of Khayyám. Khayyám's whole name was Ghiyáthuddin Abulfath Omar bin Ibráhim al-Khayyámi; Borges refers to one Al-Karnayn, who is Alexander the Great and whose presence here seems justified only by the similarity of his and Omar's names. Both stories, like the poem, mention the Sufi beggars of Islam and share an allusion to a Persian astrolabe. It is no doubt significant that those who want to destroy the house which contains the Aleph, and which "alludes infinitely to Beatriz," all have names beginning with Z, like the Zahir: Zunino, Zungri, Zunni. A Zahir destroys an Aleph anywhere.

Dante's *Divine Comedy* is satirized by innuendo in "The Aleph." Borges' mother has said that he found the poem "extraordinary." His father had made the first Spanish translation in verse of the Rubáiyát,[7] and of Omar's poem Borges wrote that "this book without equal" came into being by "a beneficent stroke of chance" (*OI*, 112; *Oth. Inq.*, 78).

Much more could be said of Borges' use of Omar, but the point does not require it. A few brief illustrations of a spiritual cor-

[6] In Omar the rose symbolizes life, youth, qualitative eternity in the present; in Dante (*Paradiso* XXXI, lines 1, 10, 19) it is a symbol of the soul's existence in Paradise.

[7] Leonor Acevedo de Borges, "Propos," *L'Herne* (Spring, 1964), p. 11.

respondence will help to show, however, that the world views of
the FitzGerald-Omar verses and of Borges' stories are essentially
the same. In the Epilogue to *Other Inquisitions* Borges writes:

On correcting the page proofs I have discovered two tendencies in the
miscellaneous writings of this volume. One, to esteem religious or
philosophical ideas for their esthetic value and even for what they contain of the singular and marvelous. This is, perhaps, an indication of an
essential skepticism (*OI*, 259; *Oth. Inq.*, 189).

This acceptance of religious and philosophical dogma only for its
esthetic value is very like Omar's:

> And this I know: whether the one True Light
> Kindle to Love, or wrath-consume me quite,
>   One Flash of It within the Tavern caught
> Better than in the Temple lost outright. (LXXVII)

Destiny, starkly present in Borges, stands out palpably in Omar:

> With Earth's first Clay They did the Last Man knead,
> And there of the Last Harvest sowed the seed:
>   And the first Morning of Creation wrote
> What the Last Dawn of reckoning shall read. (LXXIII)

Borges' oft-repeated image of God as present in all men, expressed
most clearly in his pantheistic "Everything and Nothing" (*H*,
43–45; *Dream.*, 46–47), is the same as Omar's "Master,"

> Whose secret Presence through Creation's veins
> Running Quicksilver-like eludes your pains;
>   Taking all shapes from Máh and Máhi and
> They change and perish all—but He remains. (LI)

In his poem "Luke XXXIII" Borges writes of the thief on the Cross
that he was many times thrown into sin by "bloody chance." He is
pictured as utterly predestined and completely forgiven, and his
"innocence" causes him to accept his own fate. Compare Omar:

> Oh Thou, who man of baser Earth didst make,
> And ev'n with Paradise devise the Snake:

> For all the Sin wherewith the Face of Man
> Is blacken'd—Man's forgiveness give—and take! (LXXXI)

Knowledge is impossible, Omar confirms (XXVII); and both empiricism and eschatology are empty of meaning (XIII and XXV). There is an early illusion of human individuality, but it gives way before the Oneness of all men and their identity with God:

> There is the Door to which I found no Key;
> There was the Veil through which I might not see:
>   Some little talk awhile of Me and Thee
> There was—and then no more of Thee and Me. (XXXII)

Take what comes and distract yourself, he says, until the game is over:

> As then the Tulip for her morning sup
> Of Heav'nly Vintage from the soil looks up,
>   Do you devoutly do the like, till Heav'n
> To Earth invert you—like an empty Cup. (XL)

Here is Borges' own definition of pantheism, taken from Omar:

In the Rubáiyát we read that universal history is a spectacle that God conceives, presents, and contemplates; this speculation (whose technical name is pantheism) . . . (*OI*, 112; *Oth. Inq.*, 78).

He is referring, above, to verse LII:

> A moment guessed—then back behind the Fold
> Immerst of Darkness round the Drama roll'd
>   Which, for the Pastime of Eternity,
> He doth Himself contrive, enact, behold.

And, to close a matter that could be much lengthier, here is Omar's confirmation of Borges' view that life and its contents are but a dream:

> The Revelations of Devout and Learn'd
> Who rose before us, and as Prophets burn'd,
>   Are all but Stories, which, awoke from Sleep
> They told their comrades, and to Sleep return'd. (LXV)

Coincidentally, FitzGerald's arrangement of the hundred and one verses he selected from Omar or composed himself makes the "world-dissolving" stanza ("Re-mold it nearer to the Heart's Desire") number ninety-nine, which in Borges' mythology is the number of the last utterable epithet of God, whose name is ineffable. In the hundredth verse Omar has died, and in the hundred-first the god of wine turns down an empty glass.

Is there anything in which Borges and Omar do not correspond? Omar is melancholy, spiritually rather than intellectually despairing. The spirit of the Rubáiyát is one of doubt overcome not so much by courage as by recourse to anesthesia. At this point Omar and Borges draw apart, for there is in Borges an underlying balance, a spiritual sanity which redeems him. More specifically, I would concede to Borges, as to Vaihinger, the quality of courage. Borges' "escapism" is not a flight from the world, nor is it the self-delusion of anesthesia (he attributes this function to the Zahir); it is rather a way of dealing with reality boldly and frankly. Gutiérrez Girardot has said as much: "Borges' negations, or if you wish, his nihilism, are not a rejection of the world but a positive way of knowing it and living in it."[8] In other words, there is blind courage in Borges, and where courage exists a reason for it is implied. Such positivism is faith—Tillichian faith, which has no conceivable object. Omar's esthetic is centered in the beauty of this world; but Borges' eyes have ceased to see this world. What he has seen is a something, a somehow, that is "pregnant with unformulated idea." He does not call it God, for his language is not like other men's. But he often writes of a "god behind God" and a "god beyond the gods." Again, this is not a hope of finding truth, but an intellectual esthetic: thought for thought's sake.

What I conclude is that Borges, whose esthetic is intellectual, who breaks up the world intellectually, who negates intellectually

[8] Rafael Gutiérrez Girardot, *Jorge Luis Borges: ensayo de interpretación*, p. 118.

any particular utopia or eschatological goal, and who does not hope for nor seek any mystical revelation, nevertheless does not evince the *traits* of a consciousness without hope. He does not rail or argue; he has no castle of certitude to be defended fanatically; he is not frightened, excited, bitter, or unkind. Insecure, yes, but not frantic. Borges possesses his soul. He is a veiled man who, as Asterion, has ventured out of his house; he has lifted the veil by assaying the truths of men, but has put it back on for the sake of having esthetic life. Esthesia, not the anesthesia of one or another Zahir, is sanity for Borges. There is more of reason in fantasy than in Reason itself, just as Borges' tales are more real than reality.

OTHER TRACES OF Omar can be seen throughout most of Borges'
work. The matter will not be pressed further here, except to show
the continuity between the stories discussed in the previous chapter and another significant fantasy, "The Circular Ruins," which is
also closely related to "The Cult of the Phoenix." In his poem
"Chess" ("Ajedrez") Borges credits Omar with the idea that the
chess-player who moves the pawns is himself a pawn in the hands
of a higher player. This idea is the theme of "The Circular Ruins,"
in which a magician dreams a man into reality only to discover
that he, the dreamer, is a dream in another's mind.

What does Borges mean by "dream"? This is a critical question
for anyone who approaches Borges' fiction as symbolic expression.

Let us consider a few assertions he has made in regard to *el sueño*.

In the first place, Borges' idea is the same as Descartes': existence and thought are the same thing. In speaking of Shakespeare, he equates living, dreaming, and play-acting: "The fundamental identity of existing, dreaming, and representing inspired in him famous passages" (*H*, 44; *Dream.*, 46). It is the opposition or tension between the real and the unreal worlds that produces poetry; again the dreamer and the dream are involved, as in the case of Cervantes and Quixote:

For both of them, the dreamer and the dreamed, that whole scheme was the opposition of two worlds: the unreal world of the chivalresque books and the daily, common world of the seventeenth century (*H*, 38; *Dream.*, 42).

But, he goes on to say, this same tension which died in Cervantes and his created character simply transmigrates and lives as the opposition between the now-unreal world of seventeenth-century Spain and the real world of the reader, so that "in the beginning of literature is myth, and likewise in the end" (*H*, 38; *Dream.*, 42). The myth, then, the art, lies in what Cassirer characterized as a "hovering between two worlds" (*Symbolic Forms*, II, 36). Harry Levin speaks of this limbo as the spawning ground of fiction:

The term "fabulation," which some of us have used to designate the storytelling faculty, should make clearer how the function of myth-making relates to other forms of mythmaking activity; for *la fonction fabulatrice*, as Bergson locates it, stands midway between the strictly cognitive and the vaguely intuitive, and it is out of that limbo between rational intelligence and the unconscious that fictions are generated.[1]

And, let it be repeated, "this imminence of a revelation, which does not come, is, perhaps, the esthetic phenomenon" (*OI*, 12; *Oth. Inq.*, 5).

Borges' "dream," then, is imagination, the creation of the esthetic

[1] Harry Levin, "Some Meanings of Myth," *Daedalus* (Spring, 1957), pp. 224–225.

fiction. But here I do not intend to imply only *literature*, but what C. S. Lewis has called "fantasy that hovers between the allegorical and the mythopoeic." Such fantasy is not limited to writers, as Borges would quickly agree. It is precisely because Borges' stories and prose pieces (his *thoughts*) have thought as their real subject that they are detached from mundane reality and hence are finally independent of language. Says Lewis: "The critical problem . . . is whether this art—the art of mythmaking—is a species of the literary art. . . . the Myth does not essentially exist in *words* at all."[2]

Borges' esthetic is an esthetic of the intelligence, and he usually makes dreaming equivalent to thinking—the kind of thinking, or imagination, that brings the elements of the world together into a pregnancy through extreme, almost hypnotic concentration: separation from immediate sense-perceptions and the deliberate inversion of the mind upon its contents, as if, by the heat of attention, to melt them into oneness, or to cause them to yield up something palpable, something real. In other words, dreaming or thinking is an effort to escape from language, from the idea of the world which language imposes upon us. By "dreaming" the consciousness hopes to escape its own solidified thought-history, its fixed categories, the dead words that represent memory badly and petrify the world. What the mind finally seeks is a new arrangement of reality, and to achieve this it must go back to the mythical condition prior to the gods, before language; for out of that pregnancy some more adequate God, some better language may come, though it be faceless and wordless.

That Borges does not use the word *dream* in a conventional way is obvious: ". . . at night he did not dream, or he dreamed as all men do" (*F*, 65; *Lab.*, 49; *Fic.*, 62). To dream is to dissolve solid conceptions and return to the fluidity of the mythic condition: in "The Zahir" the obsession with the coin is described to a psychiatrist as insomnia. "To sleep is to be distracted from the world" or

2 C. S. Lewis, "Preface" to *George Macdonald: An Anthology*, pp. 18–19.

"from the universe" (*F*, 126; *Lab.*, 66; *Fic.*, 115; *A*, 132). "Nineteen years he had lived as one who dreams; he beheld without seeing, heard without hearing, forgot everything or almost everything" (*F*, 122; *Lab.*, 63; *Fic.*, 112). To forget almost everything is to abstract the salient feature and forget the rest. Funes could not do this, could not think Platonically; he lay dying, a paralyzed insomniac, afflicted with "lucidity."

In "The Circular Ruins" we are taken back to the cosmogonic moment—the time of the beginning. It does not matter whether this is an objective, historical moment or a moment in the human mind—the mythic condition. Borges is driven there, in "The Maker" (*H*, 9–11; *Dream.*, 22–23), by the coming of his blindness (here intended, apparently, as the symbol of his skepticism). Speaking of Homer, but actually of himself, he embraces "love and risk" and knows that his destiny is to live in a world of his own creation—"a temple that the gods will not save"—a world of "black ships that search the sea for a beloved island." Before seeing how Borges allegorizes or symbolizes the radical regression to the mythic state, let us assure ourselves that he has a clear understanding of myth as the predogmatic, prelogical world view. In a speech made in 1945, quoted by Irby ("Structure," p. 51) and by César Fernández Moreno in his *Esquema de Borges* (pp. 29–30), Borges showed that he conceives of fantastic literature as a regression to something elemental, rather than as a horizontal ranging from reality or an upward flight:

There are those who judge that fantastic literature is a lateral *genre;* I know that it is the most ancient; I know that under whatever latitude, cosmogony and mythology are anterior to the novel of social customs.

In his short piece "A Yellow Rose" Borges deals with the discovery that drove him to skepticism: the realization that word and world are not identical:

Then the revelation occurred. Marino *saw* the rose as Adam saw it in Paradise, and felt that it was in his eternity and not in his words. . . .

Marino achieved this illumination on the eve of his death, and Homer and Dante perhaps achieved it also (*H*, 31–32; *Dream.*, 38).

Here again we are in the presence of Tennyson's flower, which is also Dante's, which is also Omar's; a Zahir beheld by Adam in the beginning, which is not in the language of men—a revelation that men receive, after which they are dead.

Borges interchanges the real and the unreal worlds. To sleep or to dream is to be conscious and thinking; to be awake, however, is to be aware of the physical world, like an automaton. "Reality was one of the configurations of dream" (*H*, 42; *Dream.*, 44)—that is, one of the contours of thought. Borges has said of "Funes the Memorious" that it is "a long metaphor for insomnia" (*F*, 115; *Fic.*, 105), insomnia being empirical lucidity, the opposite of concentrated, abstract thought. In "The Circular Ruins" the magician is afflicted with "the intolerable lucidity of insomnia" when he wants desperately to go on creating through imagination.

"The Circular Ruins" can be taken as an allegory on thought or creation. The thing created—the man who is dreamed "in minute integrity"—is an idea, a word, a poem, a fiction, a philosophical system, a self-image, or anything that is capable of being called "the truth" or reality. The act of dreaming can be conceived as the acquisition of "knowledge"—knowledge that is finally revealed to be mere illusion.

Borges is very thorough. He shows the magician returning to the mythopoeic age, or to the mythic state of mind, in order to begin the ascent toward truth. The magician's objective is to dream a man in such minute and consistent detail that he will become a part of reality. Borges takes us allegorically from the inception of thought (apprehension, hypostatization) to the final stage of full ideal being; then he shows the confirmation of this illusion when total ideal reality ("whose name is Fire") refuses to destroy the figment. The conclusion is that the thinker himself is an illusion, or from the idealist point of view, a reality. The manner in which Borges makes language more appropriate to some unnamed entity than to the ostensible subject of the narrative comprises the primary form of mythmaking, for it is the deliberate description of the behavior of the mind as if it were the objective universe, and of the contents of the mind as if they were objects in the outer world. A summary of "The Circular Ruins" follows. The story is told in the past tense, with abrupt changes into the present which may be taken as significant.

A man arrived by canoe and disembarked in the "unanimous night," kissed the "sacred mud," climbed up the river bank, and made for the circular ruins of a temple "whose god does not receive honor from men." This god is a stone statue, vaguely a tiger or a horse, and his name is Fire. The man stretched himself out below the pedestal of the statue and was forthwith *awakened* by the sun ("lo despertó el sol alto." The position of the adjective implies "the other sun, the high one," or "the sun, now high"). He sleeps, "not from weakness of the flesh, but by force of will." He knew that this was the place which "his invincible purpose required." He knew that "his immediate obligation was to dream."

The purpose that guided him was "not impossible, although it was supernatural." He wanted to dream a man and set him into reality. The uninhabited and sundered temple suited him because it "was a minimum of visible world." At first his "dreams" were chaotic; soon after, they were of a "dialectical nature." He began his task by dreaming a college of students in an amphitheater, hearing a lecture. He examined them carefully in order to select one; his selection would "redeem one of them from his condition of vain appearance and interpolate him into the real world." He was looking for "a soul worthy of participation in the universe."

He realized he could expect nothing from those students who accepted his doctrine passively (he is the lecturer), but he could take hope in those who ventured, at times, a "reasonable contradiction." The first group, although "worthy of love and affection," could not rise to the status of individuals. The latter "preexisted a little more." One afternoon he dismissed the whole college forever and kept one student, a boy whose "sharp features repeated those of the dreamer." One day the man emerged from sleep, saw the "vain light of afternoon" and mistook it for that of dawn, and "understood that he had not dreamed." He was then beset by a period of insomnia, of lucidity. He tried to reconvoke the college and failed. He comprehended that molding the incoherent and vertiginous material that comprises "dreams" is the most arduous task a man can undertake. He realized that an initial failure was inevitable. He swore to forget "the enormous hallucination" of the beginning.

I will shorten the rest of the story. In time the magician dreamed a whole man, organ by organ, hair by hair. But he was not alive. The magician appealed to the Fire god, who helped him and ordered him to send his "son" to another ruin nearby, where he would glorify the god. The newly-dreamed man would be incombustible and no one but the magician and the Fire god would know he was only a phantom. The magician complied, after erasing from the new creature's mind the memory of his long apprenticeship in the rites of the god. Before long the Fire god's ruin was razed again by fire, as it had been long before. The magician, expecting to die, walked into the flames. When they did not burn him he realized with relief, humiliation, and terror that he was only an appearance, that another was dreaming him.

Perhaps it would be best to say that "The Circular Ruins" represents the building of a concept of reality. Recognizing that the paraphrase of allegory is conjectural, I suggest the following interpretation as being consistent with the story in its entirety.

"Circular ruin" is an apt metaphor for "idealist mentality." Here it represents another kind of intellect that has essentially the same form. The circular ruin is the original, "innocent," or mythic consciousness whose "god"—whose guiding principle—is continual world-dissolution (burning, which is the method of the self-destroying, self-regenerating Phoenix). Fire is the entity that destroys; but the Fire *god* is the apotheosis of this principle, and for that reason he is symbolized in the images of the hypostat; his statue is "a tiger, a horse, a rose, a tempest." If we take "circular ruin" to signify a mental universe, the magician is a figment in this universe or macrocosm, and is himself a microcosm, a little universe peopling itself with its own creations, and these creations become objective when they are sent into other "ruins" after forgetting that they are only figments. The magician goes back to the "one-minded darkness" of psychic or historical myth in order to create, knowing that this primordial condition is necessary to thought. He kisses the primeval mud. Empirical awareness is brought about by the physical universe, the sun, but the consciousness "sleeps" (begins thinking), not from physical necessity (the objective order does not require it) but by force of will. The mind knows that its existential function, its "immediate obligation," is to think.

The purpose that guides it is not impossible, although it is "supernatural"—metempirical. Its object is to produce or reproduce reality—to hypostatize an entity which, when communicated to another "ruin," will glorify the god—the deified principle of esthetic or idealist creation. The lonely ruin is a fitting place for thought because it is a minimum of distraction and preconception. The first perceptions or thoughts are chaotic; soon after, they are of "a dialectical nature." *Dialectical* has dictionary meanings of "discriminatory" and "selective or particular." This is the point of perspectivizing or hypostatizing; the college of students represents facets of reality from which one must be extracted or elevated to supremacy. The students are attributes, one of which is to be reified.[3] The magician is looking for a "soul" or essence that deserves to be called a reality. He has hopes especially for those

[3] Vaihinger, repeating an ancient idea, says that human beings form a conception by perceiving adjectival attributes and arbitrarily making one of them a thing. This substantive entity, born as a conjecture or fiction, may be thrust into outer convention as a theory or as objective truth; later, it may regress to the status of fiction and disappear, according to a "law of ideational shifts" (*'As If,'* pp. 124–134).

facets that present "a reasonable contradiction" (Vaihinger points
out that all true fictions call contradictions into being, and that
contradiction is the sure sign of a fiction). Other attributes, which
perhaps dovetail nicely, are worthy of "love and affection," but the
more unmanageable aspects "preexist"—stand out as meaningful.
The consciousness finally dismisses the minor qualities and keeps
one "whose features repeat those of the dreamer," which puts us
again in mind of Borges' dictum that art must show a man his own
face.

The next event, which Borges says is catastrophic, may be taken
as the conversion of the half-formed idea into a hypothesis. According to Vaihinger, a fiction becomes a hypothesis when it is
taken as a possible truth. The magician mistook afternoon for
morning and thought he had not been thinking ("comprendió que
no había soñado." Borges frequently uses "understand" in the sense
of "believe," since in his view all comprehension is only belief).
That is, the magician suddenly took his past thinking for objective
perception. Thus it was that for a while afterward he remained
awake and lucid, for he was taking his imagination for reality
despite his theoretical supposition that this was an error. He tries
to get back to the beginning by recalling the whole college, but he
cannot. He swears to forget "the enormous hallucination" that led
him astray, abandons "all premeditation of dreaming," and almost
instantly is able to sleep during "a reasonable part of the day," not
noticing his dreams; that is, I suggest, not noticing *that they are
dreams*. He is able to do this by realizing that an initial distortion
or "failure" is inevitable:

. . . the task of molding the incoherent and vertiginous material of which
dreams are made is the most arduous task that a man can undertake
. . . much more arduous than weaving a rope of sand or coining the
faceless wind. He understood that an initial failure was unavoidable
(*F*, 62; *Lab.*, 47; omitted from *Fic.*).

These figures—weaving and coining—are both symbolic of hypostatization. To weave a rope of sand is to unite the elements of

being into a form; to coin the wind is to give the wind a form, a face. The first image is also suggested when Tzinacán tries to gain universal knowledge by piling up grains of sand in his dreams, and the expression "coin the faceless wind" reminds us that the Zahir is a coin.

In order to resume dreaming effectively, the magician—now that he has forgotten that his activity thus far has been a distortion of reality—restores as best he can the original mythic condition that made dreaming possible. He waits until the moon is full and round, and then he resorts to certain rites that are patently suggestive of the prescientific age. He purifies himself in the river— one of the acts which Eliade says are basic in the mythic return to the beginning. Then he worships the planetary gods, pronounces "the lawful syllables of a powerful name," and sleeps. Almost immediately he dreams of a beating heart, and the creation begins to become palpable bit by bit.

To bring the creation to life, the consciousness appeals to the will, the subjective necessity; and this "Fire god" allows the figment to live. Only the dreamer and the god will know that it is only a phantom and that fire will not consume it. The new creature is sent away. Then the fire comes to consume the circular ruins in which the magician finds that he, too, is incombustible. The reader is brought at this point to the suggestion of idealism; every truth is born of some previous, equally unreal veracity, and the chain stretches endlessly behind us. As Tzinacán is told when his mountain of dream-sand is about to suffocate him, the road he must unwalk is infinite and he will die before he awakes to reality.

I am aware, of course, that to interpret an indefinite symbol is to render it allegorical, perhaps unjustifiably. But this interpretation does not deny the possibility of others. The polyvalence or indefiniteness that we find in such stories as "The Circular Ruins" does not indicate, however, a true symbolism so much as it suggests the idealist proposition that form is prior to content. In many of Borges' stories we sense a basic form that can be given specific content on various levels of reality. What I have interpreted here as an artistic representation of the form of human ideation, containing suggestions of the history of human thought, is obviously the form also of specific mental creations, including myths, stories, poems, and other literary works. This is to say that the mental process which produces a scientific thesis, a poem, or a philosophical idea merely repeats the process which created the first god as a metaphorical representation of an abstraction. At the same time, it recapitulates the history of human thought and the making of language, which is symbolic allusion to concepts abstracted from nature. Again, this is only to say that polyvalent creations do not point to anything in nature but rather to the form of the creating intellect at the moment of creating. Borges is faithful to this idea, and his self-depicting literature is mirror-writing in which the artist sits painting his own portrait. This is not narcissism, but universalism—dehumanization and the obliteration of the self—because the artist takes himself not as an individual, but as Man. The very fact of a preoccupation with language and reality, illusion and truth, causes or at least accompanies the disappearance of the idea that a man is an individual, responsible being, for the idea of universal delusion—dreaming—greatly reduces the significance of the human personality.

I have tried to avoid attributing to Borges any kind of message, motive, or messianism. His philosophical idealism is not something he is trying to sell, but is the basic postulate of his fictional creation. I consider Borges to be "serious" in his writing only in the sense that literature itself is serious—as compared, for example, with philosophy or homily or theology. Even didactic literature with a central message to offer, or a value to uphold, tries first to sell itself as *literature*, not to impart its moral at any cost. In some degree all creative literature exists for its own sake, its own form, its own beauty; if it does not, it is not literature. Here again, in slightly different balance, form is prior to content; style is prior to material; the "music" of language is conceivably separable from words and what they stand for in the dictionary. This is to say that Mallarmé's wordless poem is a metaphor for something quite real.

In the same way that wordlessness is the condition of pure poetry, the absence of dogmas or facts—a condition of utter self-conscious ideality—is conceivably the nearest approach to truth. I would like to show, if possible, how Borges recognizes that idealism, or skepticism by any name, is itself a truth which knows itself to be a fiction. Asterion's doors are open and anyone may come in, even his destroyer. This open-minded skepticism is essential to art. I believe Borges would say that art exists in proportion to it. Those who believe this unbelievable fiction—that no-truth is truth—do so for want of an acceptable alternative, and they inevitably form a somewhat exclusive cult. Perhaps (and I think surely) Borges would agree that every real artist, every creator, every *thinker*, is a member of the cult by virtue of his ability to perceive the unspeakable mind-form whose content is infinitely variable. It is a cult to which a man is not converted by exercise of choice; it comes inevitably to the faithful—to those who stare at all Zahires, truths, dogmas, facts, and domineering ideas until they disappear because they are inadequate.

One of the most tantalizingly cryptic of Borges' prose fictions is "The Cult of the Phoenix," of which Borges says in a Prologue:

In the allegory of the Phoenix I shouldered the task of insinuating an ordinary phenomenon—the Secret—in a vacillating and gradual manner which would turn out, finally, to be unequivocal; I do not know how successful I have been (*F*, 116; *Fic.*, 105).

These little aids to the baffled reader which Borges gives in prologues, epilogues, and even within stories, are utterly ambiguous and usually have only the value of another oblique metaphor. Borges plays with his reader and knows that most of his fictions constitute puzzles that attack the mind in its most vulnerable spot: the imperious hunger for the explanation of it all. However, his brief comments do impart information; here we can take

him at his word and assume that "The Cult" is an allegory. He had
something definite in mind that is allegorized for us in this short
piece, which can be called a story only for want of a better name.

Critics commit a fundamental error when they suppose that the
definite something which Borges had in mind, and which justifies
the term "allegory," is the same thing as the secret rite alluded to
so overtly in the story. We are led astray if we attempt to decode
and interrelate the many clues, hints, symbols, metaphors, and
allusions with which Borges surrounds the Secret, as if identifying
the Secret would explain the allegory. To posit the Secret and
surround it with clues is to allegorize not the Secret but something
else; the identity of the Secret itself is immaterial. What is allegorized in "The Cult of the Phoenix" is perhaps the classical
mystery story or a Symbolist poem—or more likely, something
larger, a form, of which mystery stories and Symbolist poems are
an embodiment or a reflection. A mystery story—one of Borges'
favorite forms of literature—begins with unrelated details, builds
them slowly into a pattern or form, carries the reader to a climactic,
pregnant moment when a solution seems imminent, and then, perhaps unfortunately, puts an end to this tension by providing the
solution, usually by putting the last clue in place. A Symbolist
poem does all of this in the same way, but leaves its "mystery"
and tension unresolved in the poem itself. Borges, in writing "The
Cult," has used a compact form of the mystery story technique to
allegorize, I suggest, the creation of the esthetic situation.

Irby has suggested that this story may refer to the sex act ("The
Structure of the Stories of Jorge Luis Borges," p. 199), or more
precisely, that the sex act is the Secret of the sectarians. Others
have supported this idea by pointing to specific clues in the story,
such as Borges' observations that the rite is furtive and clandestine,
is not named in decent words, is not taught to children, causes
discomfort or embarrassment when alluded to, at first appears
shameful, vulgar, and unbelievable, and guarantees the immor-

tality of a species if the rite is executed generation after generation. But there are many more clues and suggestions that can hardly be correlated with these, and possibly no conjecture about the identity of the rite can be consistent with all of them. It is probable, in fact, that many of the hints which supposedly point to the mysterious rite called the Secret are really intended to suggest the nature of the allegory and are only collaterally related to the Secret.

If Borges did have the sex act in mind when he wrote "The Cult of the Phoenix," this would be in keeping with the structure of the story itself. The sex act, like a mystery story or a Symbolist poem, is a reflection of a larger form which embraces these three and many other phenomena. It begins in an uncoordinated diversity of gestures and actions, becomes integrated and directionalized, rises to a tension in which all movement is directed toward a climactic moment—an imminent fulfilment—and like the mystery story, at least, ends with the release of the tension. Orgasm is the death of Martín Fierro on a plain that was tense with expectancy. Fierro's killer became nobody—"or rather, he was the other one"—and Borges has observed elsewhere that in the "dizzy instant of coitus, all men are one man" (*F*, 25; *Lab.*, 12; *Fic.*, 27).

But we do Borges an injustice, we impoverish his work, if we allow the conjectural identity of the Secret to overshadow the greater values of "The Cult of the Phoenix." Whether the dark ritual is one thing or another is finally off the subject, except to the extent that the form of the Secret is like the form of the *story*.

The title of the story suggests world-dissolution. The Phoenix, about which Borges wrote in his *Manual de zoología fantástica* (in collaboration with Margarita Guerrero), is an autonomous, self-regenerating bird. Dying in fire by its own act every five hundred years, it is reborn out of its own ashes; it carries the remains of its former self to the city of the sun, in Egypt, and deposits them in the temple. In his *Manual* Borges gives special mention to the allegorical significance attributed to the Phoenix by the ancients:

The ancients believed that . . . universal history would repeat itself in
all its details . . . ; the Phoenix would become a mirror or an image of
the universe. To further the analogy, the Stoics taught that the universe
dies by fire and is reborn out of fire and that the process will have no
end and had no beginning (M, 31).

The relationship to "The Circular Ruins" is immediately evident,
but is not relevant here. Borges also tells us:

Erman writes that in the mythology of Heliopolis, the Phoenix (Benu)
is the lord of jubilees, or of long cycles of time (M, 30).

Eliade has pointed out that the psychic regression to chaos (Freud's
return to childhood, the primitive man's river-dunking, et cetera)
is the necessary condition for renewal or rebirth and that its ritual
form is often the orgy or Saturnalia. The return to primordial chaos
symbolizes for the savage the rebirth of the universe and the
beginning of a new time-cycle, and for the consciousness the
return to one's true being and the renewal of life. Eliade also shows
that the modern form of myth is seen in man's distractions, the
main form of which is reading (*Myths, Dreams and Mysteries,*
p. 37). It is difficult to think of reading as having the form and
function of orgy, but this is precisely Eliade's meaning: fiction, art,
imagination—all involve the abandonment of one's fixed world and
a movement into another, and this movement involves, however
briefly, a return to myth (chaos).

Let us suppose as a hypothesis that the secret rite of the sectarians is one which exhibits the same general form as the process
of creation depicted in "The Circular Ruins" as I have interpreted
it. The first dreams of the magician were chaotic, then dialectical,
and finally became integrated, directionalized, and in a sense climactic. This movement from heterogeneity to singularity, or from
nothing to something, is exemplary of creation. A mental construct,
a drama, a poem, a story—they all have the form of the creative
act. Besides being creative in the literal sense, and perhaps in the

psychological sense, the sex act is above all a symbolic rite, a kind of metaphysical conformity, a cosmic propriety, because it has the form of the world, so to speak. The universal form, the mind-form, repeats itself in an infinite number of phenomena, and this endless repetition reflects a familiar rhythm or cycle, a kind of gigantic respiration in the universe—or in the mind, for as Borges says, "To think . . . is the normal respiration of the intelligence" (*F*, 56; *Lab.*, 44; *Fic.*, 54). The Phoenix, with its rhythmical self-destruction and re-creation, is indeed the universe, as the ancients said.

To be more specific, then, let us suppose that the sacred ritual of the cult is the act of creating fictions—that is, thinking, imagining, dreaming—as a selfconsciously futile activity leading nowhere, justified only by an esthetic criterion. Like the primitive man's orgiastic return to chaos, dreaming is a way of renewing the world.

Among the oldest sources which refer to the sectarians by name, Borges says, are the *Saturnalia* of Flavius Josephus. The sectarians are said to be all things to all men, "like the Apostle," and to be ubiquitous. Borges hints that the reason for the "vulgar error" that associates them with the Jews is that the Jews, as Martin Buber said, are essentially pathetic. (Perhaps we may infer the Jews' being self-enclosed, skeptics from the Christian standpoint, different, wanderers in the earth, in but not of the world of other men, rather like the solipsist intellect Asterion.) At some time, we are told, there was a legend and perhaps a cosmogonic myth, but now the men of the cult have only an obscure tradition of a punishment —"a punishment, a pact, or a privilege, for the versions differ and hardly permit a glimpse of the verdict of a God who assures eternity to one clan if its men, generation after generation, execute a rite" (*F*, 183; *Lab.*, 102; *Fic.*, 165). This sentence in the original Spanish is ambiguous and is especially so if the word *fallo* is taken not in the sense of "verdict," and not as an oblique hint of "phallus" (*falo*), but in its alternate dictionary sense of something lacking to make a balanced hand of cards. In the latter case the sentence would read: ". . . hardly give a glimpse of the missing suit [or card] of a God who guarantees eternity to one clan. . . ." I interpret this to be the right idea, that the men of the Phoenix do not have a pivotal, finalizing "clue"—no last word to the poem, no ultimate solution to the mystery of the universe.[4]

The fulfilment of the rite is the only religious practice of the sectarians; the rite is itself the Secret. It is transmitted from one generation to another, but usage does not favor mothers' or priests' teaching it to children. Initiation in the mystery is the task of the lowest individuals: a slave, a beggar, or a leper acts as a mysta-gogue. One is reminded that Gautama Buddha began to think, to question the universe, at the sight of poverty and disease. Pre-sumably, mothers and priests do not customarily teach children to be skeptics; but surely slaves, lepers, and beggars are inclined to inspire such questioning. A child can indoctrinate another child in the rite, says Borges. Children are notorious for living in make-believe worlds.

The story tells us that the act is trivial and momentary and requires no description. The materials are cork, wax, and gum arabic; "Mud is mentioned in the liturgy; this also is customarily used." The meaning of these materials is highly conjectural. All are plastic or resilient substances. Taken in one sense they could all be associated with writing or the dissolution of writing, and in another sense could be connected with making things adhere. Most prob-ably, they represent materials used by actors for "making up." They alter appearances, create illusions, change faces.

---

[4] In "The Zahir" the card game in the pub is a part of the "oxymoron" that is composed of leaving Teodelina's house and going to the tavern for a drink; and at the moment of its occurrence in the narrative, Borges receives the Zahir. A Zahir, or supreme hypostat, is precisely what the sectarians do not have. A card game is symbolic of world rearrangement, just as Teodelina is symbolic of fixation. If *fallo* refers here to cards, the imagery is consistent, for the lacking suit or card would be comparable to the hundredth name of God, to Reality, to the missing link in a total vision of the universe, or to the fictional truth which men substitute for an understanding of the universe.

There are no temples dedicated to the celebration of the rite, but a ruin, a cellar, or an entrance hall is a propitious place for it. Ruins, cellars, and doorways are places of the poor and degraded; they are also symbolic of psychic humility, skepticism; and doorways, as Eliade shows, are always symbolic of the passage to another state, identity, or world.

The Secret is sacred but is also a bit ridiculous; its exercise is furtive, and the adept do not speak of it. There are no "decent" words to name it, but it is understood that all words name it, or rather, that "all words inevitably allude to it." All words, we may suppose, unavoidably point to fictions, for the world is a fiction.

In Germanic literature there are poems written by sectarians whose nominal subject is the sea or the twilight. "Sea" and "twilight" may be taken as symbols of world-dissolving powers. "Poems" may refer to kennings, those Germanic aliases for common things, which are found in profusion in the Anglo-Saxon literature of which Borges is so fond.

A kind of sacred horror prevents some of the faithful from executing the very simple rite; others despise them, but they despise themselves even more. On the other hand, much credit is enjoyed by those who deliberately renounce the Custom and achieve a direct commerce with the divinity (F, 184; Lab., 103; Fic., 165–166).

To paraphrase, some of the orthodox are prevented by "holy horror" from becoming radically skeptical of truth; others despise them, but they despise themselves more. Much credit attaches to those who renounce esthetic speculation and achieve a mystical contact with Being.

The last paragraph of the piece should be understood, I believe, as language about the adoption of the mythic point of view, or skepticism—the return to destiny, circular time, the equivocal nature of all things—as a starting point for thought and for artistic creation:

On three continents I have deserved the friendship of many devotees of the Phoenix; it seems clear to me that the Secret, at the beginning, struck them as banal, embarrassing, vulgar, and (what is even more surprising) unbelievable. They could not bring themselves to admit that their parents [*padres*] had stooped to such manipulations. The strange thing is that the Secret was not lost long ago; in spite of the vicissitudes of the orb, in spite of wars and exoduses, it reaches, tremendously, to all the faithful. Someone has not hesitated to affirm that it is now instinctive (*F*, 184–185; *Lab.*, 103–104; *Fic.*, 166).

The best commentary on this paragraph is perhaps one from Vaihinger, in which he quotes from Nietzsche's *Ueber Wahrheit und Lüge im aussermoralischen Sinne*:

"Lying, in the extra-moral sense" is what Nietzsche, with his well-known fondness for forced expressions, calls the conscious deviation from reality to be found in myth, art, metaphor, etc. The intentional adherence to illusion, in spite of the realization of its nature, is a kind of "lie in the extra-moral sense"; and "lying" is simply the conscious, intentional encouragement of illusion. . . . Art is the conscious creation of an esthetic illusion; in this sense art rests upon the "primitive longing for illusion." ('*As If*,' pp. 342–343).

If we adopt Nietzsche's forceful word "lie" in place of "think," "imagine," "dream," or "mythify," the last paragraph becomes less enigmatic. To the devotees of the Phoenix the rite—falsifying—at first appears banal, disconcerting, vulgar, and (what else?) unbelievable. They could not bring themselves to admit that their forebears had been reduced to such speculation and self-delusion. The strange thing is that arbitrary truthmaking was not lost long ago; it comes as something tremendous to all the faithful in spite of the vicissitudes of the world, wars, migrations.[5] That is, the Zahir-form comes to all, despite the forms of anarchy: vicissitude, conflict and contradiction, flux. "Someone has not hesitated to affirm" that living by self-imposed illusion—fictionmaking, esthetic dreaming—"is now instinctive." That someone is possibly Nietzsche, who said: "The construction of metaphors is the fundamental instinct of man."[6]

[5] The phrase *a despecho de las vicisitudes del orbe* could be interpreted "because of (or weaned by) the vicissitudes of the orb (eye)."

[6] Quoted by Vaihinger, '*As If*,' p. 345.

The Symbols of the Zahir

John of Panonia was burned on an upright pole sunk deep in the ground and surrounded with bundles of wood. They burned him at high noon. It was at high noon that Tzinacán was able to glimpse the spots on the skin of the tiger. It was at midday that the lightning, coming out of a rain, started the forest fire that destroyed Aurelian, John's accidental accuser. Rain preceded the first words of the Troglodyte, Homer, and signs of rain were in the sky when Martín Fierro and the Negro gaucho began their battle to the death. The careful and word-frugal Borges has not given us these details incidentally; nor is it incidental that the knowledge which Tzinacán seeks can restore a pyramid, that Funes the Memorious is "anterior to the pyramids," or that the object which drops into the world from the imaginary planet Tlön is cone-shaped and was kept in a man's belt with a handful of coins. These things are all symbols that show or accompany the form, the process, and the fact of hypostatization and of its necessary home ground, myth.

By no means are all such symbols visual, geometric, or climatic. They can also be, for example, temporal: there is a hypothetical instant in endless linear time when, for someone, the enormous Library of Babel is justified. Or they can be objective and concrete: the moment of the Library's justification corresponds to the finding of the compendious book that contains the infinite library just as Tennyson's flower contains the universe.

But the total book is not the same thing as Tennyson's flower, which contains the universe by implication; it is not the Zahir, but the Aleph—the magic orb that shows all the details of the whole Creation at a glance. There is a point in the conceptual stratosphere where the Zahir and the Aleph are the same thing, perhaps—where the Aleph is a kind of total hypostatization. But the Aleph does not really exist. Borges longs for the Alephic vision that is given only to mystics; or rather, he longs for that cerebral mysticism which is able to hypostatize all attributes simultaneously instead of successively; to do this would be to destroy linear time. But he cannot have this, and he lives by making hypostatizations, each having its distinct moment.

The tension or interplay between longed-for universality and necessary perspectivization is a recurring preoccupation in Borges, best exemplified in "The Aleph" and "The Zahir." But this interplay is not as prevalent as a more fundamental tension that we may call hypostatic rivalry: competition among the hypostatizations of the mind, or between a hypostat and its attributes. Most of the stories in *El Aleph* and *Ficciones* are (from the standpoint of motif) only variants of this form. Two ideas, two aspects of reality, two attributes or "beings" vie for the attention of the consciousness; one must be victorious over the other; so Scharlach kills Lönnrot, the Negro kills Martín Fierro, Bandeira kills Otálora, and so on. The fate of the subordinate idea is a cause for lament, in Borges' view, and although the victory of one is necessary, it is nevertheless deplorable because the victor is only a perspective, a partial image of reality. When a dominant hypostatization becomes a fixation, a dogma, it is not a rival who kills him, but the consciousness itself (the "universe"). Fire is an entity that finally tests the contents of the mind, and only the expedient and provisional beings survive. Dogmas perish because they are too fixed, too objectively real.

The symbols of the Zahir, its modifications, its opposites, and its alternatives are repeated with monotonous persistence throughout all of the stories in the two collections. In this chapter I want to introduce a number of them, to illustrate their use, and to indicate in some measure the full extent of their recurrence in Borges' fiction. A definite pattern of usage is visible.

I have already made it clear that a Zahir is an obsession representing a partial aspect of reality—a *pars* taken as a *totum*, capable of being petrified as indissoluble truth. To Borges, dogma is anathema. But this is not true of the provisional, expedient hypostatization, the truly *momentary* god, for the succession of such concepts one after another is the mind's only substitute for comprehension in the true sense of that word: total, surrounding apprehension. The provisional or modified Zahir, in other words, is the only substitute for the impossible Aleph. In Borges' scheme of things, the human consciousness must be free to choose its "gods" according to their value and the mind's necessity. He rejects dogma with scorn, he pities the formless mental anarchy of Funes, and he accepts the utility and necessity of the esthetic fiction. When the obsessive Zahir is symbolically counterposed to the Funic disorder, these opposites are compromised; out of them is hybridized, or abstracted, the provisional hypostat, the utile and meaningful "as if." This lies at the root of Borges' repeated mention of the dictum that truth arises from logical contradiction. Vaihinger said that fictions call contradictions into being; he might better have said that contradictions necessitate and allow transcending fictions.

A brief, closer look at Borges' idea of creation or ideation will be helpful. I will not illustrate it here; that will be done in examining his symbols and their uses.

The contradictory nominalism and Platonism which scholars have seen in Borges' works[1] is transcended by his idealism. Plato believed that ideas had an objective existence; Aristotle maintained that they were only convenient mental abstractions; idealism agrees with both, affirming that the useful hypostatizations of men are real and powerful forces in the world but that they do not (so far as we can tell) correspond to any ultimate or objective reality. Ideas are only imperfect reflections of external being; language imperfectly alludes to these mental forms; and the most literal expression is only conventionalized metaphor. This lack of correspondence among word, idea, and thing is in practice ignored in favor of "mythic thinking," for ideas are unavoidably expressed in language that ascribes a material, factual existence to the contents of the mind. In effect, all thinking is mythic thinking; but what we now call mythic as opposed to rational thought is ideation that is no longer conventional—the arrangement of reality in mental categories which current usage does not consider useful, perhaps not even intelligible. It is virtually impossible for most people to distinguish between what is useful and what is "true"; they attribute objective being to their ideal structures. It is for this reason, no doubt, that Borges cannot recommend that *all* men spend their time contemplating the towers of blood or the transparent tigers of Tlön. (These symbols will be interpreted in the coming pages.)

All thinking is creation in the sense that it organizes chaotic sense-perceptions in some manner, and all creation is the making of metaphor. Rational thinking uses, as half the metaphor, the entirely conventional or accepted Gestalten that have proved useful; these were once fictions but are now dogmas. When such

[1] As an example, see Jean Wahl, "Les personnes et l'impersonnel," *L'Herne* (Spring, 1964), pp. 257–264.

thinking is expressed in forms other than plain language, we call it creation in a special sense: art. Otherwise it is philosophy, science, or some other literal and prosaic mode. But thinking ceases to be rational and becomes mythic (imaginative) when it dispenses with the conventional as a part of the metaphor and forms its ideas out of Gestalten which are not "true"—i.e., when it forms *both* elements of the metaphor out of unconventional but not unintelligible hypostatizations. This utter nondependence upon dogma amounts to a total abandonment of the "real world" and a return to the flat ground of myth, where all "useless" arrangements of reality recommend themselves just as much as the familiar ones, and where all attributes lie in a horizontal equality anterior to reification. Rational thinking, or reasonable fictionmaking, differs from mythic thinking only in this, that mythic thought is original thought, lacking a conventional referent—thought that is bereft of any presupposition and whose only justification or criterion is its momentary service to the consciousness.

This rephrasing of what was said earlier has been deemed necessary for two reasons: it summarizes Borges' own clear understanding of the nature of myth, which he shows in "Pierre Menard, Author of the *Quijote*" (*F*, 45–58; *Lab.*, 36–44; *Fic.*, 45–55) and in "Parable of Cervantes and Quijote" (*H*, 38; *Dream.*, 42); and second, it emphasizes again a basic fact that must be kept constantly in mind here: that Borges' much-noticed labyrinth, his symbol for the universe, is not the objective universe but the human mind. This is recognized by critics, but only in language that betrays a general failure to accept the fact in its literalness. There is too much of conventionality in Borges criticism; commentators are forever trying to account for his words in the objective order of nature and society, precisely where they have least application.

In general, the men of Borges' stories are mythic: they are mental images that move about in the material world, acting less like men than like ideal forms. They compete for predominance in their universe, the mind. Borges' stories are full of half-formed ideas trying to become full-blown, trying to become flesh-and-blood *mental* realities. They try to displace dogmas, they try to exist despite the superiority of other pretenders, and they keep hovering about after the "universe" has turned its attention away from them, until they die. Birth and death do not correspond to physical existence and its cessation; in fact, nothing in Borges' world is truly created or born, because his world is the human intellect, which cannot create. Life begins when a man (an idea) becomes "real." Some of the men in Borges' stories never achieve reality; they never really live. Otálora, as we shall see, tried to displace Bandeira, who was "a rude divinity"; but for Bandeira, the upstart Otálora was "already dead" long before he was blasted out of the universe. Herbert Ashe of "Tlön, Uqbar, Orbis Tertius" is a walking ghost, a fading entity with a rectangular beard that used to be red. When the universe—anybody's universe—ceases to include a person, he disappears. Averroes was fulminated when Borges stopped thinking about him, just as Otto zur Linde's hand would be if God forgot it (*A*, 83; *Lab.*, 143).[2] Ordinarily, when Borges narrates events, he is not narrating events but describing the behavior of mental conceptions. Thought, he tells us in "Tlön," is a perfect synonym for the universe.

To dispense with the accepted verities and create fictions out of other fictions is to think freely in the most radical sense. It is to start from, and return to, the primordial home ground of myth in forming and re-forming one's ideas of the world. This makes it possible to see reality in many perspectives, all of them fresh and free of blinding dogmatism. If a man cannot have an Aleph, he

[2] Compare other instances of fulmination: in "Parable of the Palace" (*H*, 42; *Dream.*, 44) a labyrinth is fulminated when the exact language that describes it is pronounced; in *HE*, 33, the same words are given as the ones attributed to Otto zur Linde in "Deutsches Requiem": ". . . if the Lord's attention should wander a single second from the right hand which writes this, this hand would be plunged into nothingness as if fulminated by a fire without light"; and Stephen Albert's death in "The Garden of Forking Paths" is "a fulmination."

must at least have a panorama of views, none of which claims to be ultimate and thus blots out the rest. Borges says it all beautifully in "Pierre Menard, Author of the *Quijote*"; but to make "Pierre" clear we must first remember what happened to John of Panonia.

Borges tells us, in "The Theologians," that John was chosen to write a treatise refuting the abominable heresies of the Monotones, who believed in circular time and the repetition of all things. He did this with singular success. Years later, his rival theologian, Aurelian, was writing against the opposite heresy, an extreme nominalism which held that every moment of time was absolutely unique and contained unique material substance. Aurelian, remembering some effective words from John's old treatise that accurately described the present heresy, quoted him. John was accused by ecclesiastical authority of supporting the outlaw sect. He could have recanted without loss of integrity, since his words were written years before in a different context; but he was proud and stubborn; he refused to separate his language from his idea, or to negate the language. They executed him on a hill under the noonday sun.

An obsessive Zahir can be anything: a tiger, a blind man, an astrolabe, a compass (*A*, 103; *Lab.*, 156). It can also be a group of twenty words enclosing a thought from the past. As John was burned for clinging to his idea, we may deduce that Aurelian's quoting him was the cosmic reason for his suffering the same fate, just as Euphorbus the heresiarch was burned earlier for having stubbornly clung to his doctrine. When John and his rival Aurelian arrive in heaven, God is unable to tell them apart: "for the unfathomable divinity, he and John of Panonia . . . formed a single person" (*A*, 45; *Lab.*, 126). The form of dogma is one cosmic thing, regardless of the variation in its content. By this simple equation of each of two men with a Platonic reality Borges makes two men one; and by this means he arrives at the weird statements which draw ejaculations from critics: that all men are finally one man, that Shakespeare is somehow John Vincent Moon (because they both pretended to be someone else, thereby constituting the form of the actor), and that in the vertiginous moment of coitus all men are one man.

The burning of the three theologians is a fulfilment aimed at showing the final folly of hypostatizing when it is taken as knowledge, and is a justification of fictionmaking as the esthetic expediency of the intellect. The fictional Pierre Menard said it very well in a letter to Borges:

To think, to analyze, to invent (he also wrote to me) are not anomalous acts; they are the normal respiration of the intelligence. To glorify an occasional fulfilment of that function, to treasure up ancient and irrelevant thoughts, to remember with incredulous stupor that the *doctor universalis* had a thought, is to confess our languidness or our barbarity. Every man ought to be capable of all ideas, and I understand that in the future he will be (*F*, 56; *Lab.*, 44; *Fic.*, 54).

This is not only the manifesto of an idealist freethinker and a defense of flexible, equivocal truth, but also a demand for the radical autonomy of the consciousness. Every thinker must start at the bottom, on the mythic ground, even though he may build exactly the same structure that existed before. If he raises a conventional, pre-existent fiction, it must nevertheless be of his own manufacture, a matter of his choice in his time and circumstances, not a sacrosanct and unquestioned inheritance. This is to say that a thinker must never begin with reality, but with no-reality.

To be explicit, "Pierre Menard" shows how a literary creation can have utterly different values according to the circumstances of its creation (and Borges is not finally talking about literature, but about thought). Menard set out to compose the novel *Don Quijote* in the precise language of the original, not by memorizing it, and not by "being Cervantes," but by being that which, in Menard's time and place, would produce the identical language that was produced by Cervantes in a different time and under different conditions. To write the same thing, in the day of Nietzsche and Valéry, that was written in the day of Lope and the *autos de fe* is incredibly difficult; consequently, Borges finds the pages of Menard to be infinitely richer than those of Cervantes.

The reason for that greater richness is that Menard's work is mythic; it is totally removed from familiar, mundane reality. Cervantes, Borges writes, "opposes to the chivalresque fictions the poor, provincial reality of his country; Menard chooses as 'reality' the land of Carmen during the century of Lepanto and Lope" (F, 53; Lab., 42; Fic., 51). In other words, Cervantes contrasts the unreal with the real, but Menard contraposes two unrealities entirely removed from the here and now. Because the real world of Cervantes is not a real world for Menard, his re-creation of the Quijote is double art, mythic art. In "Tlön, Uqbar, Orbis Tertius" the literature of Uqbar is said to meet this criterion: ". . . the literature of Uqbar was of a fantastic character and . . . its epics and legends never referred to reality, but to the two imaginary regions of Mlejnas and Tlön" (F, 16; Lab., 5; Fic., 19). This double removal from the world is necessary to art, Borges believes, and it constitutes myth—that is, esthetic ambiguity: ". . . the second is almost infinitely richer. (More ambiguous, its detractors will say; but ambiguity is a richness)" (F, 54; Lab., 42; Fic., 52).

The Imagery of the Zahir

The Zahir, in the story of that name, is at first an object, then a mental image, and finally an obfuscating obsession. When we look at Borges' many alternative symbols of hypostatization, we will notice that there is very little of a concrete nature to distinguish these gradations from each other—little, that is, to tell us the difference between a dogmatized truth and a provisional hypostat. Nevertheless, the distinction is made in context. On the other hand, there are almost no distinct symbols to separate the Funes-like chaos from the idealized Aleph, nor is there much to set these apart from the "pregnant situation" or mythic condition (Borges' "hecho estético"). But again, these distinctions are made; context enables us to see how certain images may have particular and subtle values. For example, when taken out of context the same symbols must be said to represent the Zahir, the provisional hypostatization, and a full-blown idea as opposed to one which is only trying, as it were, to achieve ideal reality.

The symbols of the Zahir are clear, as are the images of a rather generalized opposite condition that we may call "universality." Again, subtlety prohibits determining, out of context, whether the latter symbols most often signify the Funes-like condition (the nominalists' objective reality, unorganized by thought), or the more positive concept of the mythic situation—the condition of imminent hypostatization.

A few—very few—of the gradations between Zahir and Aleph are evident in their own peculiar symbols. But much more often these ambiguous concepts are symbolized by combinations of images taken from both poles, or by modifications in the images of one pole or the other; consequently, there are some symbols whose grouping below is conjectural.

I must also reiterate that Zahir and Aleph are forms which must not be confused with their specific *thematic* content. They correspond, respectively, to any number of exemplary contrasts: particularity and homogeneity, linear and circular (static) time, individuality and the dissolution of the self, and so on. This contrast can be carried much farther without leaving the form; it can be applied to cultures (the mythmaking, Zahir-susceptible Germanic culture as opposed to the Greco-Latin-Oriental "universal" cultures) and to religion (prophetic, monotheistic Christianity as opposed to polytheistic Hinduism and essentially atheistic Buddhism).

In the broadest terms, the symbols of the Zahir and those concepts with which it is related or contrasted in Borges' stories can be said to cluster under the images of light, twilight, and darkness. This is not because they are all related to light and dark, but because a light-distinction is made in each of three major categories, which renders this classification convenient. I am, hereafter, using the term *Zahir* as a generic term for hypostat or perspective, regardless of whether it is provisional or dogmatic, unless it is necessary to qualify it, in which case its adjectives will make its use clear.

LIGHT. In this category are the images of the hypostat or Zahir, or those which are associated with it:

midday sun, shadowless hour (*sol alto, la hora sin sombra*)
coin, obolus, money (*moneda, óbolo, dinero; amonedar*)
point, speck (*punto*)
vertical projection or figure, especially tower or horseman; obelisk, pole (*torre, obelisco, jinete, palo,* etc.)
tree, forest (*árbol, selva, roble, acevedo;* also in English "grove"; implied in *madreselva*)
pyramid, cone (*pirámide, cono*)
rose, flower (*rosa, flor*)
bull, horse (*toro, caballo, potro*)
cards, dice, games of chance, chess (*naipes, juego, sorteo, ajedrez, suerte*)
azar (accident, chance, Providence, fate, etc.)
dream, dreaming, sleep (*sueño, soñar, dormir*)
sacredness (*sagrado,* adj.)
straight line (*línea recta*)
fixation, obsession (*idea fija, obsesión*)
railroad (*ferrovía,* "iron way")
god or gods (*dios, dioses*)
"sophisms" (*sofismas,* a synonym for ideas or truths)
sound, shout, cry (*sonido, grito*)
the color red (*rojo, carmesí, rosado;* also in names: Rufo, red-head; Lönnrot, Scharlach, etc.)
Christ (*Cristo, Jesucristo*)
tiger (*tigre, jaguar*)
path, road (*sendero, vereda, vía*)
branches, tendrils (*ramas, pámpanos*)

animals: cat, dog (*gato, perro*)
noun (*sustantivo*)
sword, dagger (*espada, puñal*)
deep wound (*puñalada profunda*)
instant in time (*momento, instante*)
singularity, uniqueness

Some of these figures are used many times; a few only once or twice, but conspicuously. Some are used to signify hypostats, and others to symbolize the very process of free ideation. Some are apparently arbitrary, some are logical in themselves, and some are conventional or literary—or mythic. For example, an animal is a logical symbol of hypostatization because, as Borges makes clear, animals live only in the present moment without past or future. A point in space or time, or a speck on the horizon, is a visual image of a something appearing in a vast nothing. A vertical figure raised above a plane represents something posed, usually, by choice or will; a bull is perhaps symbolic of will or courage—independence, hence singularity; and Christ is presented in "The Theologians" as "the straight path that saves us from the circular labyrinth in which the impious walk," or in "Tlön" as the apparent symbol of a unique and immutable entity—a dogma.

There are symbols extraneous to the groups I make here which nevertheless may accompany one or another. An example is the mirror, which is repeatedly put forward as the duplicator or multiplier of men ("sophisms") and other realities which ideally would be combined or subsumed. (This does not, by any means, exhaust the significance of mirrors in Borges' works; but the mirror, like the labyrinth, lies on a plane of symbolism above the categories I deal with here.) The mirror is often used to show the redundancy of hypostats; hypostatization is essentially form, and as Borges points out here and there, every form must be single. The specific contents of a form are finally all the same thing.

DARKNESS. Opposite to the Zahir category is that of universality or "all-seeing," which includes both the beatific or mystical vision of the Aleph and the Funic disorder or chaos, as well as the mother-ground or mythic situation. Deep darkness is often symbolic of the Funes condition or of the Aleph. Funes lived in a dark room, and the Aleph was situated in a cellar which was Daneri's photographic darkroom; it was under the nineteenth step of the stairway (nineteen seems to be one of Borges' "dark" numbers). Some of the symbols of this category are:

> circular things: circle, moon, ring, circular labyrinth (*círculo, luna, anillo, laberinto circular*)
> ashes (*ceniza*, Ashe, Ashgrove)
> dust, sand (*polvo, arena*)
> mud (*barro, cieno, fango*)
> stone (*piedra*)
> gray and yellow (*gris, amarillo, cetrino*)
> flat places: swamp, desert, plain (*ciénaga, desierto, llano, llanura, pampa*)
> deep night (*noche, oscuridad*)
> horizon (*horizonte*)
> clouds, sunlessness (*nubes, cielo nublado*)
> vacancy or omission (*omitir*)
> water, latrine (*agua, letrina*)
> wall (*muralla, muro, pared*)
> city, house, library, and other "labyrinths" (*ciudad, casa, biblioteca*, et cetera)
> defeat (*derrota*)
> fever, delirium, inebriation, vertigo (*fiebre, delirio, exultación, embriaguez, vértigo*)

In this group, aside from vertigo and its related symbols, those which seem to be used most often to indicate the mythic situation are flat places such as deserts and plains, water, the moon, vacancy, and possibly the color yellow.

TWILIGHT. This is the category of the ambiguous, the dual, and the transitional—but in a different sense from the ambiguity of the dark or mythic situation. The uncertainty or duality depicted by the images of this group is not essentially esthetic, not pregnant with promise. What is indicated here is mere change—imminent change. To this group belong original, modified, and combined images representing (1) the imminence of transition from the universal to the hypostatic or, vice versa, usually the approaching demise of a personage; (2) the rivalry of two ideas (attributes longing to be hypostats, or fictions yearning to become dogmas); and (3) the overall process of producing Zahires out of Funic disorder or primordial formlessness. Very frequently Borges distinguishes between rising and falling realities by speaking of dawn and dusk, morning and afternoon, or of daybreak as opposed to evening twilight (*el crepúsculo de la noche*).

Some of the original symbols belonging to this category, as distinguished from modified or combined symbols, are these:

fire (*fuego, llama*)
killing, shooting, stabbing
stammering, speechlessness
paralysis (this may also be classified under universality)
rivalry, duality
symmetry (*simetría*)
sadness (*triste, tristeza*)
storm (*tempestad*)
rain (*lluvia*)—this too can be classified also under universality
oxymoron, as a rhetorical concept

Some modified symbols of transition or rivalry are:

half-nakedness or disrobing
half-moon

the color orange (*azafranado, anaranjado*)
morning and afternoon sun

Combinations of images are numerous. A few typical ones are:

circular tower
speck or figure on the horizon
upright figure on a horizontal base (including a man on horseback)
tower in a garden or on a plain
oxymoron, as a concrete figure of speech

At times it is difficult to distinguish between the symbols of this category and those of darkness, myth, universality; and at times they can be mistaken for symbols of the Zahir. This is not too important if it is kept in mind that the two basic distinctions made in Borges' background imagery are the *hypostatic* and the *universal* situations—Zahir versus Aleph—with the esthetic phenomenon being a kind of momentary compromise, a hovering between the two. It would not be incorrect to say that this is an opposition between Platonic and nominalistic approaches to reality, with idealism transcending them; and that the artistic form of idealism is Symbolism.

The symbols of the twilight group present other, more subtle problems. At times they seem to be used to differentiate between provisional and objective (dogmatized) realities. Certain specific images are problematical: seeing both sides of a coin simultaneously is, in "The Zahir," symbolic of advanced obsession, a state in which the Zahir is taken for an Aleph; elsewhere this is perhaps indicative of ambiguity. Quadrangular things are the opposite, in a sense, of circular; hence they indicate hypostatization, but they seem to be associated only with fading and disappearing beings.

A special and important case is the color *red*. I have listed it under the images of the Zahir, rather than here, although it seems to be used most often in connection with hopeful or would-be hypostats or to indicate the former reality of something now being forgotten, as in the case of men who have faded red beards or who live in houses that were formerly red and are now only rose-colored, or in the case of men who lose blood.

Some images consisting of a noun and an adjective are oxy-moronic mixed symbols. "The Lottery in Babylon" depicts the whole process of human thought as if the mind were a lottery; the citizens of Babylon are ideas living by the caprice of an ideational mechanism as it is motivated by desire, will, and irrationality. These citizens make contact with "the Company" (the authority that operates the mental lottery) by leaving bits of information in "certain stone lions," in "dusty waterways," and in "a sacred latrine named Qaphqa." Each of these three figures combines a symbol of the Zahir with an image of universality: lion combined with stone; the idea of path or way combined with water and dust; and sacredness combined with latrine. The implication is that access to the Company is gained through sense perception (the modification of objective reality) or through the making of hypostatizations upon a mythic base—that is, through conscious fictions. A clearer image, in "The Library of Babel," is of "old men who for long periods hid themselves in the latrines, with some metal disks in a prohibited dicebox, and feebly imitated the divine disorder" (*F*, 91; *Lab.*, 56; *Fic.*, 84). The metal disks, coins, may be taken as realities in a mind. But here the image of water is our concern. Water is symbolic of objective reality prior to thought-distortion; to make water is to return to mythic, primeval reality or to mental anarchy—to imitate the divine disorder. In other words, these old men whose minds are boxes of shifting and variable ideas are of the same clan as the veiled men of Babylon who mutter blasphe-mous conjectures in the twilight. In "The Approach to Almotásim" the student who is looking for the ultimate, a pure form, comes upon a dirty old man urinating (imitating the divine disorder) by *moonlight* atop a *circular tower* situated behind a *wall* in a *dis-orderly garden* beyond a couple of *railways*. This multiplication of symbolic elements suggests the tenuous nature of fictionmaking in the midst of chaos; the dirty old man is somehow akin to Tzinacán in the moment when he is suffocating under his pile of dream-sand, for in the search for knowledge he has reached the top of a tower of truth whose circularity shows its conjectural nature, and there he is trying to duplicate the mythic situation just as the magician of "The Circular Ruins" tried to reconvoke the college of students. The old man's act of urinating by dim moonlight contrasts with the student's happy arrival at knowledge, symbolized by light of an intense kind; he enters through Almotásim's curtain, behind which is a resplendence (*resplandor*).

It goes without saying that the images and figures listed in these three categories do not comprise a complete tally, and perhaps not more than a beginning toward one. A comprehensive list would embrace almost every other line of every story, and my purpose is not so much to enumerate these symbols as to show the pattern to which they point. I have omitted many, and no doubt there are many that escape me.

One group of symbols which may include referents to all of the classes above should be mentioned here in order that we may refer to it later. Borges extinguishes most of his protagonists, and does so in a limited number of ways. Among those who are despatched by shooting are these noteworthy personages:

> Loewenthal of "Emma Zunz"
> Otálora of "The Dead Man"
> Hladík of "The Secret Miracle"
> zur Linde of "Deutsches Requiem" (who is to be shot)
> the false Villari of "The Wait"
> Lönnrot of "Death and the Compass"
> Pedro Damián of "The Other Death" (in one version of his death)
> John Vincent Moon (or his nameless adversary) in "The Shape of the Sword" (this is debatable)

Stephen Albert of "The Garden of Forking Paths"
Kilpatrick of "Theme of the Traitor and the Hero"

—not to mention the clucking gods of "Ragnarök." A few persons die of knife wounds:

Abenjacán (or Zaid?) of "Abenjacán el Bojarí" (we cannot be certain that either did)
Yarmolinsky and Azevedo of "Death and the Compass"
Martín Fierro in "The End"
Dahlmann of "The South" (presumably)

Glencairn of "The Man on the Threshold" is beheaded by a lunatic with a sword. Funes dies of "pulmonary congestion," as does Pedro Damián in one version of his death—and as did, incidentally, the infamous Lazarus Morell in *Historia universal de la infamia.*[3]

Herbert Ashe of "Tlön" and Nils Runeberg of "Three Versions of Judas" die of ruptured aneurisms (loss of blood); Emma Zunz's father, Maier, takes an overdose of veronal; and Teodelina Villar and her counterpart, Beatriz Viterbo, simply die. But John of Panonia, Aurelian, and Euphorbus are burned.

The manner of death is probably without particular significance in some of these cases. But shooting, occasionally stabbing, seems to be the preferred and perhaps invariable fate of the pretender to "godhood"—the nothing that wants to be something or the entity that has come into rivalry with another that it cannot displace. Burning seems to be an extreme that is resorted to in the effort to dissolve dogmas; fire, as I have said, is to be associated with the action of the consciousness in getting rid of its fixations. The flames

[3] A note appended to "The Library of Babel" tells us that the number of men in the infinite library has been reduced by suicide and "pulmonary diseases." Apparently Borges equates thinking with living (he states the equation here and there; see *OI,* 35; *Oth. Inq.,* 20–21), and living with breathing (cf. "Pierre Menard," where thinking and inventing are called respiration of the intelligence). Thus problems of ideation, or the inability to know, are seen as difficulty in breathing—lung congestion.

did not harm the magician of the circular ruins because he was not a fixation; he was a pure fiction, and in the end a conscious one. Death by ruptured aneurism came to Nils Runeberg and Herbert Ashe, and these men also share an allusion to the fact that they are not too well remembered. They are both fading into nullity; Runeberg's first name suggests *nil* or *nihil,* and Ashe's surname suggests all that is left of the Phoenix. Ashes are among the symbols of universality, which is a kind of nothingness.

The monotonously recurring symbols of the Zahir and the Aleph, besides being an indication, possibly, of what Borges modestly calls "'my fundamental poverty" (*AP,* 7; *Per., ix*), are allusions to something he would like to express and in my opinion does express very well: the universe as a mental process, and what it means to be a Tlön-making sectarian of the Phoenix. The object here is not to illustrate or name all of the symbols, but only to show that they do have an incidence and a meaning.

The Unqualified Hypostat

The symbols of the Zahir as an unqualified, rigid hypostatization do not occur as commonly as my thesis may imply; this is because Borges does not wish to be redundant. When his subject is dogmatic truth or strong idea, he often omits the more obvious symbols of it. Such symbols are used mainly in contrast or oxymoron with others to show modifications and relationships and to depict the ideality of our facts about the world. In "The Zahir," the main story in which we might expect to find such concrete images as pyramids, pyres, suns, and other hypostat-symbols, we find instead a subtler kind, most often verbal and conceptual.

Teodelina Villar, whose first name suggests "little goddess," was looking for the absolute "in the momentary." Her "arbitrary and unauthorized caprices" are participating symbols of hypostatization; they have as their counterparts the successive "faces" assumed by her dead countenance during the wake. She left off being a model because she was running into competition from "insubstantial little girls." She "crowned a hierarchy" and "lacked imagination," she was stolid, and it is possible that her death is called a solecism simply because dogmas hardly die. She is a very concrete sort of person, and when Borges leaves her "rigid among the flowers" he goes immediately into circumstances which symbolize the opposite of the Zahir. It is the middle of the night; the low, one-storied houses have taken on "that abstract air which they customarily take on at night." Borges is "drunk with an almost impersonal piety."

Having made a kind of oxymoron of situation, Borges brings up the subject of oxymoron. Defining it, he offers examples—*dark light* and *black sun*—both of which combine basic symbols of Zahir and Aleph. He then says that leaving Teodelina's house and buying a caña (an alcoholic drink) comprises oxymoron, adding that the circumstance is augmented by the fact that some men were playing cards. The *caña*, like his pious inebriation, is a symbol of universality; Teodelina is the Zahir; *naipes* (cards) are a symbol of provisional hypostatization, for an indefinite number of Gestalten can be formed by rearranging the cards. The oxymoron here is actually a three-sided symbolism which completely expresses Borges' idea of the world. In "The Aleph," Daneri's long, universal, Aleph-like poem wins a literary prize, while Borges' own entry is rejected; the latter is entitled *The Cards of the Gambler*, undoubtedly a metaphor for "the conjectural truths of the idealist."

Borges bought an orange caña. Yellow is symbolic of the universal or primordial; red is one of the more important symbols of hypostatization; combined, they make orange. In his change Borges receives the coin which is the Zahir. He goes on to inform us that the Zahir is one of the ninety-nine epithets of God (of the universe)—one of the innumerable perspectives thereof. One Zahir in history was destroyed "so that men would not forget the universe." When one has seen a Zahir, it is said, "Verily he has looked on the tiger,"[4] which signifies obsessive insanity or sainthood. The

---

[4] Occasionally Borges inserts an English sentence into a story; this is one.

All-merciful does not allow more than one thing at a time to be a Zahir; that is, the mind sees reality in a single aspect: obsession with plural realities would be a paralyzing ambiguity, as it is with Recabarren in "The End" and with Funes. Tennyson's flower is mentioned as being analogous to the Zahir; also the rose, in contrast to the veil. The latter image (*velo, cortina*) signifies the problem of knowledge or understanding which in effect is overcome by the Zahir. The rose seems to be presented here as genuine truth, not just the illusion of knowledge, for it is said that the Zahir is "the shadow of the rose and the rending of the veil." But this is tenuous and would be inconsistent with Borges' general philosophy.

The symbols are more concrete when we go on to "The Theologians." In the first few lines the contrast between the universal and the particular is variously shown. The monastic library (Aleph) is invaded by the Huns on horseback (Zahir), whose god is an iron scimitar (Zahir). They burn everything, but a fragment of one book is rescued from the ashes (Aleph). This book is the twelfth book of the *Civitas Dei* (Aleph). The extreme subtlety of Borges' symbolism, shown in these oxymora, forces me to call each pair of words (monastic library, Huns on horses, iron scimitar) either Zahir or Aleph; but actually, each pair is a contrast in itself, of such delicacy that Zahir or Aleph emerges predominant but not exclusive. For example: *monastic* suggests oneness and isolation, while *library* is a universe-symbol; a monastic library is a universe made up of particular things, hypostats—or it is an isolated collection of ideas, a mind. *Hun* suggests the barbaric and primeval; a Hun on horseback is a Zahir-symbol, but somehow the mythic universe itself is hypostatized in the image. *Iron* is a strong Zahir-symbol, but the half-moon shape of the scimitar modifies it; in the end, what emerges as the god of the Huns is the same pantheism (iron scimitar) that characterized the polytheistic religion of Droctulft the Lombard ("History of the Warrior and the Captive"). The burning of the library by the Huns and the salvation of a fragment of the "duodecimal book" is reminiscent of the holocaust in the circular ruins, which spared only the unreal magician.

No doubt a connection is to be made between the twelfth book of the *Civitas Dei* and Herbert Ashe of "Tlön," who was preoccupied with the duodecimal system. In "The Theologians" the duodecimal book is the one which promulgates the heresy of circular time and the eternal return, and this heresy causes the circle (Aleph) to replace the Cross (Zahir); that is, cosmic destiny becomes dominant over ideas of prophetic, linear time and all that it implies of personal responsibility. Aurelian writes against the heretics and heaps upon them the symbols of repetition and confusion: "he compared them . . . with that king of Thebes who saw two suns, with stammering, parrots, mirrors, echoes, capstan mules, and bicornute syllogisms." These images are all symbols of a universe of multiplied, heterogeneous objects, the cosmic confusion of redundancy that is overcome by the Zahir.

The opposite heresy of the Histriones—in one phase an extreme Zahirism—replaces the Cross with the mirror and the coin (obolus). That is, a supreme hypostat is replaced with a "mere" hypostat and a mirror to duplicate it. The names applied to the Histriones show their predication of airy unrealities as real: they are called Simulacra, Speculars, Forms, Abysmals, and Cainites. The difference between these "straight-liners," as we may call them, and the "circulars" of the other heresy is essentially that of Platonism and nominalism. The "circulars" are mythic, nominalistic; the "straights" are Platonic, believing in forms. Borges points out that the runic cross combines cross and circle and represents a balanced view (of reality). But most important of all the alternative names for the straight-line Histriones is one that suggests the reason for the deaths of so many of Borges' protagonists in other stories: Cainites. Where hypostats are redundant, murder or the subordination of attributes is imminent, for all thinking is aimed at simplifying the universe. In showing that the redundancy of nominalism is hardly different from the superfluity of Platonism, Borges reveals his intimate understanding of these concepts which are transcended in idealism, and he justifies Eliade's otherwise contradictory assertion that Plato, with his forms, summarized the worldview of archaic (mythic) man. This is the same as saying that nominalism and Platonism are but two aspects of a single reality; the human mind hypostatizes on both the concrete and the abstract planes. An object and a form that subsumes objects are both hypostatizations.

The condemned theologian John of Panonia groveled and screamed in the dust; again a mixed or oxymoronic symbol, for dust is an emblem of the primordial or universal, while screaming (sound) is hypostatic. Asterion's redeemer will rise above the dust, remember, and in "Averroes' Search" we will see the dust contrasted visually with the vertical tower formed by a boy standing on another's shoulders. After John is consumed under the noonday sun, Aurelian goes away and seeks to comprehend his destiny; he seeks therefore the places symbolic of comprehensiveness: "the sluggish swamps and the contemplative deserts, where solitude would help him"—that is, flat places propitious for the formation of an aloneness (singularity) of idea, an upright knowledge. He dies (knowledge is death) when a vertical and instantaneous (hypostatic) bolt of lightning cuts through the rain and sets fire to the trees. Here, as in "The Circular Ruins," the forest is representative of a universe of hypostatized, redundant things. Unlike the magician, who was an ideal figment, John is unable to withstand the flames.

Dogmatism or the objectification and petrification of a fiction is the character-giving idea of "The Theologians," and the inversion of this idea underlies "The Circular Ruins." In "The Dead Man" we have the case of a would-be hypostat, Otálora, trying to come into being, to "crown the hierarchy" at the expense of the god now dominating it, Azevedo Bandeira. Otálora is "a sad *compadrito* [Argentine Cockney] with no other virtue than an infatuation with courage." Borges connects the idea of courage, hope, or will with that of making fictions, after the manner of Schopenhauer's philosophy. Otálora goes out into the "equestrian deserts" (a mixed image: we may infer "the place where ideas begin") to join Bandeira's band of smugglers. Right away we are told that he will die "in his law, by gunfire." Bandeira (cf. *bandera*, flag), whom Borges describes in his Epilogue (*A*, 171), is a "rude divinity." His first name, Azevedo, was possibly the name of one of Borges' ancestors (cf. *acevedo*, which Borges says is a kind of tree;[5] *acebo* means holly). He is said in the story to give the unjustifiable impression of being *contrahecho* (double meaning: hunchbacked, counterfeit; I interpret "false" or "ideal," capable of being displaced in the variable universe). Otálora joins the band "with the sun already high" after meeting Bandeira the night before. He sees the chief's red-haired mistress, red-colored horse, and tiger-skin saddle trappings, which are the "attributes or adjectives" of Bandeira. In an interview Bandeira offers Otálora a *caña* to drink and also offers him a job. Let us infer: he offers him the symbol of nonpreeminence and a position as Bandeira's underling. Otálora accepts. Then his "life" begins, appropriately described in terms that signify the birth of a potential hypostat: "a distinct life, a life of vast dawns and of workdays that have the odor of the horse." This life, we are told, is "in his blood." Blood is Borges' frequent symbol for courage, will, life; it participates in the highly important redness that almost always accompanies a personage who represents the real or potentially real, as opposed to the gray of the has-been and the yellow of the dead or universal. Symbols of the universal or mythic occur now, followed by references to horsemanship, sleep, storm, freezing, and sound:

He learns to ride horseback, to round up the stock, to butcher, to handle the lasso that holds the tripping balls, to resist sleep, storms, freezes and the sun, to giddap with a whistle and a shout (*A*, 29; *Per*., 28).

[5] Borges furnishes this clue in an interview; see Ronald Christ, "Jorge Luis Borges," *The Paris Review*, No. 40 (1967), p. 162. The dictionary yields only *acebedo*, a grove of holly bushes.

This sentence is loaded with double meanings. *Entropillar la hacienda,* to round up the stock, bears a tenuous overtone of "to lord it over the ranch" (*entropillar* means *entablar caballerías; entablar,* in one of its common meanings, is *fanfarronear,* to swagger or bluster. To lord it over the *horses* or remudas would be an action halfway to Otálora's eventual goal). But at the same time Otálora learns to resist the impulse to usurp Bandeira's place too soon; all the things he resists are symbols of hypostatization: sleep, storm, freeze, sun. Learning to handle the tripping balls (*boleadoras*) suggests Otálora's purpose, which is to overthrow Bandeira. The other images (whistle, shout) are hypostatic symbols, and *carnear* (to butcher) is suggestive of the shedding of blood, which usually occurs in Borges' stories with the demise of a dominant figure; in "The Lottery in Babylon" the narrator cuts the throats of sacred bulls, and in "Emma Zunz" the issue of blood from Loewenthal's body is the signal of his hierarchical demotion.

But this beginning of "life" for Otálora is quickly brought into question when Bandeira is mentioned again; they say of him, with regard to any other man's show of prowess, that Bandeira does it better. This suggestion of the chief's vertical preeminence is placed immediately on a horizontal base; he was born beyond the Cuareim, and this "obscurely enriches him with populous forests, swamps, and inextricable and almost infinite distances."

Then occurs a scene that is packed with the symbols of the Zahir, its redundancy, and the life-and-death cycle of all hypostats. Bandeira is sick and it befalls Otálora to take him his supper. The room where the chief is lying is disorderly and dark. On one wall there is "a remote mirror with a moon-shaped tarnish." The sick Bandeira, horizontal on his bed, is outlined by "a vehemence of dying sun." The big white bed seems to make him darker and smaller. Among these indications of the apparent decline of the god there appear others that indicate the possibly imminent rise of Otálora to a status of full being: in the mirror he sees the red-haired mistress. It is fitting that she should appear as a mere reflection, for she also carries the visual marks of the half-Zahir: she is half-dressed and barefoot. But Bandeira, the apparently faded entity, suddenly sits up, and while he gives orders and makes plans he plays with his mistress's red hair.

The band then goes to a place on the "interminable plain," without trees, where the flatness is beaten "by the first and the last sun." We get the feeling that this is a place where gods are made and unmade in the course of a day. Otálora has been rather reckless and obvious in his desire to rival Bandeira; consequently, Bandeira's newly-acquired bodyguard now enters the story ominously. He comes as a "shadowy horseman" and his name is Ulpiano Suárez (*ul*, Arabic "of"; *piano*, Italian "flat"). He is primeval, let us say —mythic—and has the power to make or unmake Otálora. In Borges' symbolism "shadowy horseman" is an oxymoronic combination of darkness and uprightness indicating a purely ideal being, the kind that the cosmic fire will not burn. Suárez is a bearded man, which in Borges' scheme means that he is real. Otálora knows he must win this man, and he tries, telling him of his plan to overthrow the chief.

One day, appropriately at high noon, Otálora manages to usurp Bandeira's place at the head of his band during a skirmish; that afternoon he rides the chief's red horse back to camp and drips blood from a wound onto the tiger-skin saddle blanket; and that night he sleeps with the red-haired girl. He has thus possessed all of the "attributes" of the reality he wants to become. These attributes, however, are themselves hypostats, for they are symbols in themselves—red, horse, tiger; which means that Otálora aspires to crown a whole structure of being. The "pregnant situation" that he hopes to climax is on a high level; Bandeira is, after all, a "rude god." We can predict at this point of the story that the symbols of the esthetic crescendo will soon appear.

Otálora has stopped taking Bandeira's orders. One night—a night mixed with alcohol, and with a guitar in the background— Otálora is drunk and celebrating: ". . . he erects exultation upon exultation, jubilation upon jubilation; this tower of vertigoes is a symbol of his irresistible destiny" (A, 33; Per., 31). A tower of dizzinesses (not a dizzy tower) is a Babel of hypostatizations. Every hypostat rises out of a "pregnancy," and a series of these pregnancies produces the illusory structure of man's reality, which is finally his hope or his will; and it was Otálora's destiny as a man to build this tower of illusions, just as the magician's "immediate obligation" was to dream.

Otálora comprehends, before dying, that from the beginning he has been betrayed . . . because they already considered him dead, because for Bandeira he was already dead. Suárez, almost with disdain, fires (A, 33; Per., 32).

But although Otálora is a man, he is also an idea in a mind, like the magician, like Averroes. Borges does nothing casually or accidentally, and the last word of the story—fire ("hace *fuego*")—is deliberately chosen. It recalls the fire of the circular ruins, the theologians, and the Phoenix.

Redness and the "Twilight Zone"

With these images—sun, darkness, plain, blood, et cetera—behind us, it will be easier to show the same pattern of symbolism in other stories and to do so more succinctly. First it will be helpful to discuss the meaning of the color red in its generality, because it is more prominent in other stories than in those already mentioned. Quite often redness is used in combination with symbols of the twilight condition or the imminent dissolution of reality rather than with those which indicate a near-hypostatization. Most of the time it is used in contexts which indicate simply the ambiguity of rivalry or the half-real nature of a personage. Sometimes it is used to show that a hypostatization is provisional and "real" as opposed to one which is dogmatic and therefore dead or doomed.

The discussion of "The Circular Ruins" and "The Cult of the Phoenix" in the previous chapter pointed out some of the symbols to be associated with the Phoenix: fire, sun, ashes, mud, et cetera.

In the former story also appear the moon, the night, the color yellow, and mentions of tiger, horse, rose, bull, storm, coining, a reddish sky, and a "red Adam."

Also in "The Cult of the Phoenix" are these lines:

> May the Nine Firmaments know that God
> Is as delightful as the Cork and the Slime.
> (F, 184; Lab., 103; Fic., 166)

The swamp or moor (ciénaga) figures among the symbols of the mythic situation, as I shall show; here, cieno (slime) is given the same value as the légamo (mud, clay) of the secret rite or the fango (mud) which the magician, "the gray man," kissed upon arriving at the circular ruins. These lines contrapose mysticism and myth (or idealism) and affirm that they are equally delectable.

Both these stories have to do, as I said, with the dissolution and creation of ideal reality. They contain the symbols of both the mythic situation and hypostatization in a way that shows the properly provisional nature of fictionmaking.

Tamayo and Ruiz-Díaz have shown (Borges, enigma y clave, pp. 39 ff.) not only that Borges often uses names suggestively but that in "Death and the Compass" in particular, the names of the antagonists are "loaded." The color red, they point out, is visible in Red Scharlach (Scharlach is German for scarlet) and in Erik Lönnrot (rot is German for red). They do not mention that Erik is also suggestive of Eric the Red. The color is also present in the story in other forms, such as bloodstains. What Tamayo and Ruiz-Díaz conclude from this does not seem to go beyond the idea that Borges used the color red to give a hint of the cosmic identity of the two men. On the contrary, I think it indicates their immediate, ideal lack of identity; or, to put it better, they are two hypostatizations which for one reason or another—perhaps their near identity—cannot both exist. Tamayo and Ruiz-Díaz rightly conclude that the whole story is a conflict between reality and an interpretation of it, if we accept their way of saying it, and that Red Scharlach is able to trap and kill Lönnrot because the latter has a false idea: his interpretation of the case he is investigating is the right one, and yet is not complete in spite of its logical completeness and coherence. In other words, Lönnrot falls victim to a dogmatized partial aspect.

Lönnrot represents an idea that wishes to prevail. Scharlach represents another. They are in rivalry[6] and this is symbolized by mixed images suggesting intolerable ambiguity and the impending dissolution of a hypostat: redness, blood, grayness, half-nakedness, two deep knife wounds, sundown, twilight, dawn, east and west, gods of two faces (one of whom looks at both dawn and dusk), duality in other forms ("two eyes, two hands, two lungs, are as monstrous as two faces"), symmetry, and sadness.

Aside from these emblems of equivocality, there are clear symbols of the hypostat: tower, Cross, sword, dogs, horse, light, the name Azevedo, and others. And finally, apart from them all, are the symbols of the Funic chaos, the Aleph, and the mythic situation: waters the color of the desert, a sphere of crystal, the horizon, a circular yellow moon, the "gods of fever and mirrors," and more.

Redness is often employed in oxymoron to show the twilight ambiguity, as in this sentence from "The Circular Ruins":

In the Gnostic cosmologies, the demiurges knead a red Adam that cannot stand up; as inept and crude and elemental as that Adam of dust was the dream-Adam that the magician's nights had fabricated (F, 63; Lab., 48; Fic., 62).

"Red Adam" is a mixed image: Adam is a symbol of the primordial passivity, while red is suggestive of life.[7] The unsuccessful Adam is also an "Adam of dust." He lacks the fire of a conscious-

---

[6] Each wants to "persist in his being," as Spinoza phrased the basic drive of the human consciousness. In a way that is typical of him, Borges casually throws into the story a mention of "Baruj Spinoza," who has no visible connection with the story or its contents.

[7] According to Borges, the name Adam means "red earth" in Hebrew. See Ronald Christ's "Jorge Luis Borges," p. 127.

ness that needs or wants him. The magician's dream-son is just as unsuccessful, until the fire god animates him. This god tautologically combines many symbols of hypostatization; he is "not . . . an atrocious hybrid of tiger and colt, but those two creatures and also a bull, a rose, a storm" (*F*, 63; *Lab.*, 48; *Fic.*, 60–61). In other words, this god of reality is really real. But the last figure in the group—storm—stands for imminent change, or the possibility of change; this modification testifies again to the ideality or provisional nature of the mental universe.

Let us look quickly at other red things: in "The Zahir" there are red rings in the Niebelungs' treasure; in "The Library of Babel" the hexagons of the infinite library symbolize the universe, and the red hexagon is the one in which the compendious books (those that imply more than themselves) are found; a thief in "The Lottery in Babylon" steals a red ticket, by which action he hopes to rise in the world. Also in "Lottery," the narrator—an attribute—has a red tattoo that subjects him to a continual shifting of rank in the ideal hierarchy:

. . . a vermilion tattoo: it is the second symbol, Beth. This letter, on nights of a full moon, gives me power over men whose mark is Ghimel, but subordinates me to those with Aleph, who on moonless nights owe obedience to those with Ghimel (*F*, 67; *Lab.*, 30; *Fic.*, 65).

Many stories have blood in them, the most unusual being "History of the Warrior and the Captive," in which the captive English girl jumps off a horse on the plain and drinks the blood of a slain animal. In "Averroes' Search" the black-haired slave girls torture a red-haired slave; this is mentioned just at the moment of Averroes' error, when an imperfect idea is formulated by him and taken for the truth. There is red wallpaper in "The Wait," and a red circle around the moon in "The End." The tavern where Dahlmann is challenged by the man who will kill him, in "The South," used to be a deep scarlet, just as Herbert Ashe's rectangular beard ("Tlön") used to be red. There are many other such examples, as we shall see.

Provisional Hypostatization

There is redness in "Tlön" of a type which shows (at least in this story) its symbolism of provisional hypostatization or the making of ideas on a basis of utility or esthetic volition. The theme of "Tlön" is simply the creation of ideal reality from the ground up. Tlön is an imaginary planet, without a word of "truth" in it, which is so much more esthetically useful than the planet Earth that the material world finally begins to assume the form of Tlön; or rather, the form Tlön, for Tlön is only form. In this story we see not only the symbols of the Zahir modified by those of the Aleph but also the pure images of the hypostat (tower, et cetera) modified in such a way that the intention to depict the self-defining, free, and undogmatic fiction is made clear. In Tlön there are transparent tigers and towers of blood.

The tiger is an unmistakable hypostatic symbol. The words *tiger* and *tower* would be enough to signal fictionmaking here, but Borges' purpose is to show the ideal nature of it; *tiger* is a strong symbol, and when made transparent it is given the character of ideality without being weakened. *Tower* is strong too. Blood, as I have said, often symbolizes human strength or courage—the will to create or be created. A tower of blood is therefore a double or reinforced image of hypostatization based on volition and has the same force as the new *Quijote* of Pierre Menard: it suggests radical ideality, mythical art, the fantastic.[8]

The one most outstanding feature of the planet Tlön is, of course, that it has no dogmas. It is one vast, organized structure of provisional ideation. We could call it the Promised Land of the sectarians of the Phoenix. The Secret ritual—the making of aboriginal fictions—is alluded to by many words (even as Borges said in "The

[8] I am aware that there is possibly phallic symbolism in Borges, particularly in his use of the tower image. But such an interpretation of any of his symbols would lie entirely outside the pattern I am trying to describe. In any case, I would contend that "phallic symbolism" is a misnomer and that Borges merely uses symbols that are subject to interpretation as phallic.

Cult": all words inevitably allude to it—presumably because all words refer to hypostatized *things*). For example, "Tlön" gives us these:

Noun: "There are no substantives in the conjectural *Ursprache* of Tlön, from which come the 'present' languages and the dialects: there are impersonal verbs . . ." (*F*, 20; *Lab.*, 8; *Fic.*, 23). In the language of the northern hemisphere, the basic unit of speech is the monosyllabic adjective, and nouns are made of accumulated adjectives: ". . . the mass of adjectives corresponds to a real object; the fact is purely fortuitous" (*F*, 21; *Lab.*, 9; *Fic.*, 23). In Tlön nobody believes that such nouns refer to real things, and this proliferates them: "The fact that possibly nobody believes in nouns causes, paradoxically, their number to be interminable" (*F*, 22; *Lab.*, 9; *Fic.*, 24).

Aspect: "They know that a system is nothing but the subordination of all the aspects of the universe to any one of them" (*F*, 23; *Lab.*, 10; *Fic.*, 25).

Object or *idea*: ". . . ideal objects abound, convoked and dissolved in a moment, according to poetic necessity. Mere simultaneity at times determines them" (*F*, 21; *Lab.*, 9; *Fic.*, 24).

Law: "At the beginning it was believed that Tlön was a mere chaos, an irresponsible license of the imagination; now it is known that it is a world and that the intimate laws which govern it have been formulated, even though in a provisional way" (*F*, 20; *Lab.*, 8; *Fic.*, 22).

We could go on, but the purpose will be served as well if we only look at some of the incidental symbols of the hypostat appearing in the story. The people of Uqbar, the germinal predecessor of Tlön, left obelisks where they had lived, and stone mirrors. Borges uses the idea of the duplication of reality by reflection to signify that all hypostatizations are but duplications of a single form (men themselves are, in mythic thought, only particularized manifestations of a single and eternal life-substance). Bioy Casares discovered the original sentence which led to the revelation of Tlön:

Copulation and mirrors are abominable because they multiply the number of men. The metaphysicians of Tlön do not seek truth, but astonishment (just as the idealist and the mythic thinker seek to save the world from banality), and philosophical systems abound because they are all dialectical games; they are incredible, "but their architecture is agreeable or of a sensational sort" (*F*, 23; *Lab.*, 10; *Fic.*, 25).

Other symbols of particularization and the rejection of dogma are less obvious. It is consistent that Ezra Buckley, the reprobate millionaire who financed the invention of Tlön, required that the project have nothing to do with "that impostor, Jesus Christ," for we may presume that Jesus, when taken as the Christ, is the archetype of dogmatized uniqueness and final reality. Another less obvious allusion, subjected to controversy in the story—is the thrice-mentioned problem of the present moment as related to others. The first allusion is metaphorical: it comes under the guise of the problem of the other volumes of the Encyclopedia:

In the "eleventh volume" of which I speak there are allusions to subsequent and preceding volumes. Néstor Ibarra . . . has denied that those fellow volumes exist (*F*, 19; *Lab.*, 7; *Fic.*, 22).

The second is theoretical:

To explain (or to judge) a phenomenon is to relate it to another; that vinculation, in Tlön, is a posterior state of the subject which cannot affect or illuminate the former state. Every mental state is irreducible: the mere fact of naming it—*id est*, of classifying it—amounts to a falsification (*F*, 22; *Lab.*, 10; *Fic.*, 25).

And the third is clearer; it questions the validity of subjecting "all the aspects of the universe to any one of them" on the grounds that this "supposes the impossible addition of the present instant and all the past instants" (*F*, 23; *Lab.*, 10; *Fic.*, 25).

This is, of course, the nominalist insistence that general ideas are a falsification. But here it consitutes only another of Borges' devices for furthering his idea that the creations of the mind are inevitably fraught with logical contradictions which prove their value and point beyond them to something not yet seen; for, as Vaihinger said, "contradictory ideas are there only to be finally eliminated" ('As If,' 98). The inherent paradox of every truth merely asks to be transcended. This, I believe, points to the meaning of the obscure third entity of the story: Orbis Tertius. Only the combination of opposites can produce transcendence; the uniting of like things does not require it. At the end of "Tlön" the counter-position of the fictional world of Tlön and our own "real" world begins to result in the conformity of the material world to the Tlönic pattern. But in another sense, Tlön is pure idea of the Platonic type, while the world is matter—the nominalists' objective reality prior to thought. What Borges means to convey, I think, is that out of the juxtaposition of Tlön and Earth (idealism and empiricism) comes a third world, an Orbis Tertius. Tlön represents absolute idealism, or solipsism, but the third orb will represent the modified, tenable idealism which holds that the universe as we know it is half objective, half our idea. The conformity of Earth to Tlön is already accomplished in a philosophy of "as if." Such a philosophy is aptly metaphorized as a transparent tiger, since it is a self-acknowledged heuristic fiction that makes no claim to ultimacy.

Most clearly illustrative of hypostatization is the *hrön* (plural, *hrönir*) of Tlön. The hrönir are described as material objects—which means that they are ideal objects, for in Tlön matter does not exist. As the story puts it, they are objects produced to replace lost objects. We are told that until a short time ago they were the casual children of distraction or forgetfulness, and that it seems unbelievable that their methodical reproduction dates back hardly a hundred years. A hrön can be an *ur*, an object produced by suggestion or hope; it is then a purer and stranger object than an ordinary hrön. A hrön, in other words, is a hypostatization—something "made up" which replaces a made-up entity that is lost, and it was hardly a century ago that men began to produce these things *sys-*

tematically. I suggest at least one analogy: fantasy, or imagination, did indeed occur in literature as a relatively nonserious and *unmethodical* mode until about a century ago, when Symbolism was begotten by Poe and Baudelaire and those who followed them.[9]

The subject of Tlön is deep and almost inexhaustible. I will cite no further examples of its symbolism except in connection with that problematical personage, Herbert Ashe. Ashe is the taciturn, shadowy Englishman whose purpose in the story is difficult to discern unless he is taken as nothing more than a container in which to drop the conventional symbols of fading reality—that is, unless he is the symbol of the world which is sure to pass away under the influence of Tlön. His name, Ashe, suggests this dissolution, as well as the transformation of the Phoenix, which rises again out of the ashes of its former body. Ashe is characterized as "suffering from unreality," and he periodically goes to England to visit "a sundial and some oak trees," just as the Phoenix flies off every half-millenium to the city of the sun. Ashe is given the aspect of a grayish sort of man; he has a "tired, rectangular beard that was formerly

[9] Many affinities between Borges and the Symbolists that could have been commented on in this study have been passed over. This one deserves a note. The hrönir are called secondary objects, and elsewhere in the story, in connection with language, we are told that certain "second grade objects" can be combined with others and that the process is infinite. "There are famous poems composed of a single enormous word. This word constitutes a *poetic object* created by the author" (*F*, 21; *Lab.*, 9; *Fic.*, 24). This harks back to Borges' idea of myth as being a third entity based on two unrealities in juxtaposition, and looks forward to the vertiginous tower of illusions of Otálora and the pile of infinite grains of sand in Tzinacán's dream. But it also reflects the Symbolist idea of the slow evocation of an object by metaphorical, never direct, allusion. In "The Zahir" and elsewhere Borges speaks of the repetition of the ninety-nine epithets of God, who presumably exists as, and is evoked by, his hundredth name. If this name were a familiar one, like Yahweh, the Symbolists would claim that speaking it would "kill" God as a reality. The mythic thinker would agree. In such a case the hundredth name would be a summation of the epithets. But if the name were unknown, speaking it would wreak inconceivable havoc, possibly fulminating the conceptual universe.

red." When he dies of a ruptured aneurism he is said to be "less a ghost in death than he was in life." The memory of him in the Hotel Adrogué is now limited and diminished, in the same fashion as that of his fellow nonentity, Nils Runeberg of "Three Versions of Judas," who "will perhaps be remembered." This fading memory of a faded man persists among the "effusive honeysuckles [*madre-selvas*: etymologically, "forest mother" or "mother forests"] and in the illusory depths of the mirrors" (*F*, 17; *Lab.*, 6; *Fic.*, 20). He had been an engineer on the southern railways. Shortly before his death Ashe received in the mail and left in the bar the eleventh volume of the Encyclopedia of Tlön.

Ashe is a reality that ceased to exist. Redness has left his beard, which is quadrangular. Rectangularity is to be taken, it seems, to indicate that a mere outline remains of something that was. In "'The Garden of Forking Paths," Yu Tsun is shown a letter written by his ancestor, a man "of my blood" who no longer lives; it is "a paper formerly red, now rose-colored and tenuous and quarter-creased [*cuadriculado*]" (*F*, 106; *Lab.*, 25; *Fic.*, 97). The beard is a hypostat symbol; rectangularity turns it into the symbol of an insipidity, a cliché, or an archaism; and indeed, Borges pictures Ashe as an unprovocative, tasteless man. Taken as a whole, Ashe is a prefiguration of the story's conclusion: a reality is ceding to another and better idea.

The Mythic Situation

Each of the stories mentioned as exemplifying the basic theme of hypostatic rivalry (and this includes the Aleph-Zahir contrast) employs the same conceptual forms or elements, but places a different emphasis upon one or another. The story which best symbolizes the pregnant or mythic situation is perhaps "The End." A brief interpretation of this story was given in the first chapter; here I must elaborate on it in order to show the use of symbols.

The story, as I have said, is a fictional addition to the gaucho epic *Martín Fierro* by José Hernández. The gaucho Fierro has returned to the general store on the pampa where, seven years before, he killed a Negro gaucho in a fight with knives. He has met the brother of the dead man and defeated him in a *payada de contrapunto*, the music contest of the gauchos, a dialogue in counterpoint to guitar accompaniment. Fierro leaves, but the Negro remains for several days at the store, knowing that Fierro has recognized him and will come back. When he does return, they fight and the Negro kills him. All of this takes place before the eyes of Recabarren, the proprietor of the store.

Recabarren represents the human mind, paralyzed and inarticulate in the face of ambiguity. He suffered a stroke just after the gauchos met in the contest of counterpoint. As the story opens he is waking up from an afternoon nap. He hears a guitar being played by the Negro; the music is "a kind of very poor labyrinth which tangled and untangled itself infinitely." Recabarren is "accustomed to living in the present, like the animals," and now he looks at the sky and sees "the red circle of the moon," which he takes to be an indication of coming rain.

The plain under the "last sun" is almost abstract. A point moves on the horizon and grows until it becomes a rider headed for the store. We already know which of the gauchos will survive, because the Negro first appeared when Recabarren woke up—when there was still "much light in the sky." Fierro appears with the dying sun. Fierro arrives, converses a while with the other gaucho, and reveals that he has told his children "man should not shed the blood of man." They go out onto the plain to fight; the exact spot does not matter to them: "one place on the plain was like any other and the moon was shining." Indeed, in Borges' plan, when the moon is shining, when the world is flat or circular, or when it is dark, everything is equal to everything else. The fight begins.

At this point Borges gives us the sentence that is almost a repetition of his definition of the esthetic phenomenon: "There is an hour in the afternoon when the plain [*llanura*: flatness] is about to say something" (*F*, 180; *Fic.*, 162).

The guitar music, the "poor labyrinth," is symbolic of the cosmic confusion. Recabarren is accustomed to living by the hypostatization of time: in the present moment only. He looks at the red circle around the moon and expects rain. The moon and circularity are indicative of the universal oneness that underlies the seeming heterogeneity of the world; redness here signifies a modification of the meaning of the circle, and rain is to be associated with imminent change; in other words, there is going to be a passage from the mythic, esthetic condition to something else. The plain is going to yield up a palpable form to replace the ambiguity. But it will not be the esthetic fulfillment, the perfection promised or implied in the ambiguity; it can only be a short-circuit resulting in a "word." With regard to the rain image, we shall see later that the Troglodyte (Homer) of "The Immortal" loses the power of speech, regains it during a rainstorm, leaves off being universal and immortal, and goes in search of his mortal singularity.

The coming of Fierro is described in the image of an enlarging speck on the horizon—a form in the midst of formlessness. When he arrives there are two men, two realities, contending for unique existence. Why must one of them die? Why must the mind of Recabarren contain only one of them? This is Borges' question, the whole question raised by the tension between Aleph and Zahir. As Borges says elsewhere, two things exactly alike cannot exist (*H,* 42; *Dream.,* 45); every ideal being must be singular. Borges' antagonists are often declared—by critics, at times by Borges—to be somehow the same person. But why must this annihilation take place? Why can men not see all perspectives and contain all ideas? Martín Fierro has told his children that man ought not to spill the blood of man; let us say, ideal figments ought not to have to murder each other for the sake of the singularity of forms. This is reminiscent of Menard's pronouncement that all men should be capable of all ideas, and also suggests the theme of "The Garden of Forking Paths," in which a wonderful book has been written which preserves all destinies, all the alternate possibilities that could result from events in the plot. Borges could lament, with Rodó, that man is afflicted with "the most abominable of inferiorities . . . a brain incapable of reflecting more than a partial appearance of things" (*Ariel*, p. 45). But the longed-for Alephic vision is denied Recabarren. When he woke up, earlier, he was awake forever to that form of mind which hypostatizes and then cannot lose or change its realities—awake, that is, to the daylight condition: he returned to "daily things that he would no longer exchange for others" (*F*, 177; *Fic.*, 159).

The fight begins out on the plain under a moon that is not qualified by an adjective. The emphasis is upon the dim light it gives: "the moon was shining" (*la luna resplandecía*). Because it is the moon that gives it, this light is not like the brilliance, the *resplandor*, that came from behind the curtain of Almotásim. The small "knowledge," the poor fulfilment that is about to take place on the pampa, will hardly resemble the revelation that came to Tzinacán in the moment when he was illumined by the light from the trapdoor that opened at high noon.

Fierro is finished when he receives a deep thrust. Yarmolinsky and Azevedo also die of "puñaladas profundas" in "Death and the Compass." Just as a hypostatic reality is often symbolized by sharp things—projections, swords, daggers, upright figures, obelisks—the liquidation of a reality is usually accomplished by a puncture caused by a bullet or a blade. This shows a dry, laconic, technical humor in Borges. Congested men die of congestion; broken men die of broken blood vessels. So definitive, closed-up beings must perish just as fittingly, by being opened up, having holes put in them. Borges makes the emphatic point in "The Cult of the Phoenix" that the sectarians have never suffered persecution. This is undoubtedly because they do not make or comprise dogmas which have to be shot, stabbed, or burned![10]

[10] Compare an aspect of the extreme individualism of the Mexican, as described by Octavio Paz in *El laberinto de la soledad*, pp. 55–74; the concept of *chingón* and *chingado* is comparable, on the emotional plane, to this intel-

The indefinite, polyvalent poem was ended when Fierro died and the Negro was, so to speak, canonized. He became a form which subsumed his rival: ". . . now he was nobody; or rather, he was the other one." We may suppose that Recabarren regained his movement and his speech and continued about his "daily things."

Sentential Symbols of the Hypostat

Much more subtle that the symbols that appear as sound, color, visual form, or time-concept are the verbal or situational images that show a correspondence to the pyramidal or hierarchical structure of ideation. I will give only a handful of examples here, since others will be mentioned in the following chapter.

In "The Lottery in Babylon" the winners of each drawing may be compared to the momentary gods or egregious realities of a provisional Gestalt. But they cannot be momentarily victorious—cannot "crown the hierarchy" like Teodelina—unless the losers in the lottery, the momentarily subordinate realities, are willing to pay the fines corresponding to the losing tickets. If the forgotten attributes, in other words, refuse to be forgotten, the hypostatizations cannot materialize. The Funic chaos prevails. This story will be discussed more fully in the coming pages.

Another such example is the statement, in "History of the Warrior and the Captive," that Droctulft, up to the time of his "conversion," had been "loyal to captain and tribe, but not to the universe" (A, 48; Lab., 128). A directionalized emotional attitude has

---

lectual rivalry of ideal realities. The *chingado* is the person who "se raja," who opens up; the *chingón* is the one who causes this ignominious opening. As Paz points out, the idea of *chingar* is not finally a sexual allusion, but metaphysical; no doubt its correspondence to forms of nature and anatomy has caused these words to become indecent. We might remember in this regard that the continual creation and destruction of hypostatizations is (perhaps) the secret of the sectarians and that there are "no decent words to name it." Could Borges have had in mind a correspondence to the concept described by Paz? It is universal in Spanish America. Paz's discussion of the point may be read in English in *The Labyrinth of Solitude,* pp. 74–88.

the same ideal form as particularization on any other plane of being. The image is accompanied by concrete symbols: forests and coins.

The form of hypostatization is present also in the statement that Tadeo Isidoro Cruz "saw his own face . . . heard his name" (A, 55). The preterite tense, of course, is hypostatic whenever it appears in the context of the imperfect; but the point here is not grammatical. The context of the action is a lifetime; the momentary and egregious reality is a sudden clarity of vision or self-understanding. The concrete symbol is again present: the word *noche* (night) is given six times in five lines to form the background time of the event (A, 55). The words *instante* and *momento* are posed against the background of *siempre* (always).

Omissions are often symbols of ideational focus, as in the case of *fallo* (read *falta,* lack) in "The Cult of the Phoenix," where the image perhaps suggests the lack of an element that would complete a Gestalt (F, 183; *Lab.,* 102; *Fic.,* 164). Another such omission is in "Tlön, Uqbar, Orbis Tertius," where Bioy Casares delivers a polemic about a novel in the first person "whose narrator would omit or disfigure the events and fall into various contradictions, which would permit a few readers—a very few readers—to guess an atrocious or banal reality" (F, 13; *Lab.,* 3; *Fic.,* 17). An omission or contradiction that permits the perception of a truth is only technically different from a revelatory image or fact. The sentence immediately following the one quoted above informs us that a mirror was spying on the conversation; if Borges is true to form here, the implication is that there is something to be reflected, though nothing reflectable has been mentioned.

To name another example quickly, there is the circumstance that the protagonist of "The Wait," when asked his name, could think of none but that of his enemy—the name, that is, of his rival, Villari. The concrete symbols surrounding this statement are profuse. The story will be taken up in the next chapter.

And finally, an "omission" of a much more fanciful kind is given

us in "The Garden of Forking Paths." In order to make the identity
of an English city stand out so that the Luftwaffe can bomb it, Yu
Tsun is compelled to murder—to *omit*—a man of the same name.
The totality of the omission—the reduction of Stephen Albert to
ideal nothingness—is indicated by the word Borges reserves especially for this purpose; his death was "una fulminación" (*F*, 110;
Lab., 29; *Fic.*, 101).

The Recurrence of the Motif

$\mathcal{I}$ HAVE BEEN TRYING to describe what I consider to be Borges'
central motif, the impulse-giving Form that underlies his short
story creations. I have attributed to him, mostly for reasons of con-
venience, a consciousness and a deliberate use of the concepts of
hypostatization and its necessary ground, the mythic condition.
Actually, I do not contend that this usage is altogether conscious,
though I feel it surely must be. Nor do I pretend that Borges
would understand or agree with the particular terminology that I
apply here to describe his symbol system and what it signifies.
Furthermore, it is obvious to me that Borges' fictional work can be
spoken of just as appropriately in purely *thematic* terms: as al-

legories and symbols for literary creation, as stories about circular and linear time, as tales of finitude and infinity, as problems of individuality and homogeneity, as puzzles involving personal identity and "nihilism," as stories about order and chaos, as artistic expressions of a philosophy of knowing and not knowing.

But when we speak of Borges' work in such thematic terms, it is difficult to show anything in the nature of an underlying continuity or unity beyond the fact that the subject matter recurs sporadically. It is perfectly correct to say that "Death and the Compass" is a detective story à la Chesterton, or that it is a clever interweaving of mathematical concepts, or that it proves Borges to be erudite in matters of philosophy and theology. But the recurring symbols in this and his other stories are not, by and large, connected with the content, subjects, or themes of these fictions. They can be associated only with the pervading motif or thought-form that repeats itself in story after story. It is the aim of this study to do nothing more than point out, in the simplest language possible, that this thought-form is visible.

The purpose of this final chapter is to show how the motif can be seen in the remaining stories of *El Aleph* and *Ficciones*. First I must justify, briefly, the assertion that this form is single.

The opposition of Aleph and Zahir may take the thematic forms mentioned above. The idea of hypostatic rivalry may be expressed as human competition or animosity, physical combat, murder, intrigue, pursuit, and flight, or as indecision and conjecture. Simple hypostatization has two faces in Borges: original ideation "from the ground up," as in the case of the man-dreaming magician, or attempted duplication of ideal reality, as in the case of Averroes' trying to conceive "comedy" and tragedy" (and Borges' trying to conceive Averroes). In these cases hypostatization is depicted in the form of men thinking, but it can also be expressed as men acting, as in the case of Otálora. Thus we have three motifs: hypostatization, hypostatic rivalry, and the counterposition of Zahirism and universality.

But there are stories in which more than one of these is present. For example: Lönnrot is trying to displace Scharlach; this is rivalry. Like Averroes or Pierre Menard, he is trying to duplicate adequately the ideational process or mental configuration of another man; this falls under the heading of simple hypostatization. In another sense, Lönnrot is trying to reduce a reality to nothingness by becoming identical with it—by being unique Form, which in Platonic terms must exist singly. Scharlach, meanwhile, is trying to avoid being reduced, duplicated, annihilated. The battle takes place against a background in which the symbols of the primordial mythic condition are proliferated and suggest that the action is happening on a stage or in some other realm where the reader sees all: the reader is given a kind of Aleph.

For these reasons I call the motif single. It is necessary that I make this clear for this reason: although "Death and the Compass," for example, bears no superficial resemblance to "The Theologians," and neither of them to "The House of Asterion," these stories and the others previously discussed can be reduced to a common terminology and shown to spring from one or another emphasis within the form I have described.

So without attempting to categorize further, I will take up the remaining stories in the order which I feel is most appropriate for the effective demonstration of my thesis.

I have referred to many of the thirty-four stories in *El Aleph* and *Ficciones*. The following eight are those which I think have been dealt with adequately in the foregoing pages:

The Zahir
The Aleph
Tlön, Uqbar, Orbis Tertius
The Theologians
The Dead Man
Pierre Menard, Author of the *Quijote*
The Circular Ruins
The Cult of the Phoenix

Some of these will be mentioned again, only to point out aspects and symbols not included in preceding pages. Twenty-seven stories remain, most of which will have to be discussed much more briefly than the subject and the material warrant.

I must add that to identify a motif, or even the themes which correspond to it and carry it out, is not to say that the whole narrative has been accounted for or defined. There is much more in Borges' stories than his symbolism and the thread of the narrative: criticism, asides, philosophy, sophistry, capricious detail, exquisite language, parable, illustration, exegesis.

"The Lottery in Babylon"

In the first paragraph of "The Lottery in Babylon" we are given a symbolic or allegorical foreword to a coming description of the free-thinking, world-dissolving intellect. It is the intellect of Asterion, analogous to that of Shakespeare the play-actor who is "everything and nothing" (*H*, 43–45; *Dream.*, 46–47). Borges takes us through a history of the development of human thought (under the guise of a history of the lottery), gives us a pithy and complex description of the activity of an idealist mentality that grows more idealist before our eyes, and then corroborates, in the last paragraph, that the thing which has been elaborately metaphorized for us is indeed the human consciousness. The mind, which is a mass of collected perceptions or knowledge, is "omnipotent"—i.e., the world is whatever the mind makes it. Despite this omnipotence, the mind's influence upon outer reality is limited to certain things, according to one conjecture offered by Borges:

Another conjecture declares that the Company is omnipotent but that it has influence only in miniscule things: in the cry of a bird, in the hues of rust and dust, in the half-dreams of dawn (*F*, 75; *Lab.*, 35; *Fic.*, 71).

These small things over which the omnipotent mind holds sway are symbols of the Zahir and of myth: sound (cry), shades of red, dreams or half-dreams, the shades of dust. The mind has power only in regard to the degree or type of its hypostatizations upon a base that is mythic in one or another degree.

Another view, Borges says, holds that the mind is nothing but an endless construction, dissolution, and reconstruction of Gestalten:

Another, no less vile, reasons that it is irrelevant to affirm or deny the reality of the shadowy corporation, because Babylon is nothing more than an infinite interplay of accidents (*F*, 75; *Lab.*, 35; *Fic.*, 72).

At the beginning of the story the narrator assumes, in describing himself, the behavior pattern of an image in the mind; that is, of an aspect of reality which is alternately dominant or subordinate in its Gestalten according to criteria that Borges symbolizes in his conventional way, through images of redness, hope, bull, two opposing kinds of twilight, night, moon, cellar, blackness, stone, and others. Under the light-condition necessary for hypostatization, symbolized here by moonlessness (daylight is used for another purpose), the narrator dominates other men. But when there is a moon, he is subordinated and in fact is forgotten completely; during a lunar year he was declared invisible and nobody heard him when he shouted or punished him when he stole. The red tattoo that subjects him to this condition is a letter, Beth; and Asterion, remember, does not know the difference between one letter and another—hence their free alternation here. The tattoo is vermilion, and the condition to which it subjects the narrator is equated with "what the Greeks do not know: incertitude" (*F*, 67; *Lab.*, 30; *Fic.*, 65). This uncertainty is ideality; as Borges says in his *History of Eternity*, "for the Greeks a substantive name without some corporeality was impossible" (*HE*, 81).

In the half-light of dawn, which indicates the imminent rise of a hypostat, the narrator has cut the jugular veins of sacred bulls.

That is, he has diminished the substance (drained the blood) of fixed realities; his rise as an ideal reality is accomplished at the cost of others. This rite is performed— i.e., these other realities are subjugated by him—on a stone, representing the primordial mythic ground, which is black like the "unanimous night" of the circular ruins; and it is in a cellar, like the Aleph and like the clandestine practice of the Secret. The recurrent rising and falling of the hypostat, the narrator, occurs between the night and the day, the time when all realities are changed; but his existence is placed against a background of moonlit and moonless nights, which means that he is not to be confused with any kind of "truth." He is a mental reality that we would call a mere figment of the imagination, otherwise Borges would probably have him exist in the daylight.

The second paragraph begins to identify the country (the mind) in which the narrator-figment lives; its most distinguishing feature is the lottery. The lottery, or the process by which the mind functions, is the system through which all the other "men" in Babylon are subjected to the same ups and downs as the narrator: all have been proconsul; all have been slaves; all have known omnipotence, opprobrium, jail. The free dissolution and reconstruction of being (the lottery) is "a fundamental part of reality" in Babylon, but in other republics (minds, philosophies) it is almost unknown or functions imperfectly and secretly. The lottery, obviously, is endless fictionmaking, for Babylon is where "veiled men murmur blasphemous conjectures in the twilight" (F, 68; Lab., 31; Fic., 66).

Borges confesses that he knows as little of the purposes or meaning of the lottery as a man who is ignorant of astronomy knows about the moon. He has not sought out its history. But he offers a conjectural history, beginning with what his "father" told him about the old days. The rest of the story is a development by parable of the idealist philosophy, ending in a description of Borges' own pattern of thought and perhaps of his mode of literary creation.

In the third paragraph Borges brings us, as if from a generalized prologue, into a narration of specifics, changing his symbolism to sunlight and coins. His description of the beginning of the lottery is suggestive of the time, before philosophy, when there was no dichotomy between language and reality—when mythic thinking prevailed:

My father used to say that in ancient times . . . the lottery in Babylon was a game of plebeian character. He said (and I don't know whether he was right) that barbers dispensed, in return for copper coins, rectangles of bone or parchment adorned with symbols. In broad daylight a drawing was held: the fortunate received, without any other corroboration of chance, minted coins of silver. The procedure was elemental, as you see (*F*, 68; *Lab.*, 31; *Fic.*, 66).

The reason why Borges saved the symbol of daylight becomes apparent. The drawings that took place in the early, elementary lottery happened "in full daylight," which we may take to mean that the ideas (the "winners") raised up in the mind were not known to be fictions but were taken as literal truth. The winners were rewarded with *minted* coins of silver (or coins minted of silver: *monedas acuñadas de plata*; in any case an implication that the *copper* coins were not man-made), without any other "corroboration of chance." The word for chance, *azar*, must be taken in a special sense throughout the story; it means, vaguely, "objective reality"—but this will not serve, for in mythical thought all reality is objective and to the idealist it is all, or nearly all, subjective. These opposite words or concepts are the same in effect, for they both drive reality into one or another place in relation to language. *Azar* must finally be equated with the substantive use of the verb *acertar* (to hit the mark); *azar* has the value of *acierto*. "Chance" is finally "correctness" in the sense of Vaihinger's "usefulness," which is subjectively determined. This "chance" denies the possibility of any outside "corroboration."

The citizens taking part in the lottery paid *copper* coins, symbolic of a stage of being inferior to, or prior to, that of full being, which is symbolized by coins of *silver* minted by the consciousness. They received rectangular pieces of bone or parchment. As in the case of Ashe's beard, a rectangular shape signifies a state of half being. The whole image suggests dice and playing cards (instruments of chance) or lottery tickets,[1] and reminds us of the title of the book written by the Borges of "The Aleph": *The Cards of the Gambler.* "Citizens" who do not take part in the Babylonian lottery are called cowards and are scorned; they are insignificant attributes not worthy of hypostatization.[2] This phase of the lottery is called plebeian and elementary because it does not really represent a free play of thought since it considers image and outer reality to be identical; every configuration of mind is taken as authentic. For this reason, surely, Borges uses quotation marks when he tells us that "those 'lotteries' were a failure."

The failure of the early lottery is attributed to the fact that it did not direct itself to all of man's faculties, but only to hope. Again, this testifies to a principle of mythic (primitive) thought. In the childhood of a race, or of an individual human being, there is little objective, rational fictionmaking as distinguished from imagination or "poetry." Everything conceivable or expressible is taken as truth, and truth is the expected result of each "drawing." To say that the lottery was directed at man's hope is to say that it was not esthetically motivated, not skeptical, not idealist.

Later the lottery began to include not only winning tickets but

[1] Critics have observed that barbers sell lottery tickets in Buenos Aires. The tendency is to seek an identification between Buenos Aires and Babylon. There is none, except to the extent that Buenos Aires corresponds in form to an idealist intellect. Such a thing would be hard to show, though there is an obvious comparison to be made between a city and a labyrinth.

[2] Note the similarity to the parable of the coins told by Jesus. The Babylonians surrender their half-being (copper) and take a chance on becoming "real." In the parable, the pusillanimous servant buries his coins for fear of losing them, is judged guilty by reason of cowardice, and has them taken away and given to the more audacious. The final dictum is consistent: "To him who has shall more be given, and from him who has not shall be taken away even what he has." The idea is the same as "He who will save his life (his being) will lose it."

also tickets that awarded a fine; they took away, that is, what little coin (being) the losers already had. This is to say that the subordinated attributes were further submerged in the hierarchy of being, to the greater glory of the winner, the hypostat. We might call this the stage of dogmatism, of cruel and unyielding conviction.

With fascinating precision Borges moves on. The hypostatization cannot be made unless the losers are sufficiently yielding. But the losers become rebellious and refuse to pay their fines, preferring to go to jail "in order to defraud the Company." Here it becomes clear that the thing defrauded, the Company, is Knowledge or Certitude: singularity of idea—Truth. "Jail" *(cárcel, prisión)* is used to show that the subordinated realities—the connotations or attributes appended to the hypostat—are no longer utterly submerged and forgotten, but are held in abeyance for a limited period. This is the beginning of free thought or imagination, the time in our individual or collective thought-history when the ideal-objective dichotomy appears; the jailbirds are not destroyed but will again play in the lottery when the next shuffle of reality may make them momentary winners. We are told that the "bravata" of these jailbirds who refuse to surrender their coin is the source of the Company's omnipotence (its power to operate the lottery, to make and remake reality) and of its "ecclesiastical, metaphysical virtue." Let us paraphrase: the continual recognition of connotation as the possibility of varied perspective makes metaphysical speculation possible; and connotation—the vaporous overtones of language and life that are not contained full-bodied in the Name of a hypostatized reality—are what gives things their sacred or religious aura. Until the god is born out of the "pregnant situation" he is only connoted by the visible elements. The esthetic reality is a religious and metaphysical reality.

Knowledge, or the Company—the ideational mechanism—soon sheds its dogmatic nature. It began to withhold the publication of fines and to announce only jail sentences. That is, hypostats stopped losing their connotations; gods became Gestalten. This was "of capital importance"—undoubtedly because it was the maturation of the fictionalizing faculty. "It was the first appearance in the lottery of non-pecuniary elements," or the first recognition that the lottery involved language, so to speak, that had far more to it than was evident in mere dictionary definitions. Success was great, and the Company had to increase the number of adverse tickets. Paraphrased: the increased value attached to imaginative connotation caused an increase in the number of "wrong" or "useless" ideas: a proliferation of fantasy, as distinguished from fact. Perhaps this is the point at which Symbolism of the French kind is born, in which the figment arises as the meritorious rival of the fact.[3]

Here is Borges' clear statement of the principle and value of esthetic imagination or the destruction of conventional and useful hypostats: "Some moralists reasoned that the possession of coins does not always determine happiness and that other forms of felicity are perhaps more direct" (F, 69–70; Lab., 32; Fic., 67). Conventional ideas, in other words, are not necessarily the right ones —or better, "right" ideas are not always the most beneficial or useful. The words felicidad and dicha are well chosen, for beauty and convention are not necessarily the same thing. This is Borges' philosophical and artistic manifesto, mildly stated.

At this point we have merely walked through the door into "The Lottery in Babylon." The remainder of the story is much more subtle and complex. It continues to be a description of the idealist mentality (or of the human mentality as seen by an idealist), but it moves in the direction of an allegory on artistic creation as such. Recognizing this, I will nevertheless continue in the same fundamental terms.

Let me attempt first to clarify the meaning, as I see it, of a difficult passage of great import:

. . . one must remember that the individuals of the Company were (and

[3] Vaihinger distinguishes between useful or scientific fictions and those which are useful in the esthetic sense; for these "artistic" fictions he prefers the name figment ('As If,' p. 81 n).

are) all-powerful and astute. In many cases the knowledge that certain felicities were simply fabrications of chance would have diminished their virtue; to avoid that objection, the agents of the Company employed suggestions and magic. Their steps, their manipulations, were secret. To inquire into the intimate hopes and the intimate terrors of each citizen, they had astrologers and spies at their disposal. There were certain stone lions, there was a sacred latrine named Qaphqa, there were some cracks in a dusty aqueduct which, according to general opinion, *led to the Company;* malignant or benevolent people deposited accusations in those places. An alphabetical archive collected these notices of variable veracity.

Incredibly, mutterings soon followed. The Company, with its customary discretion, did not reply directly. It preferred to scrawl in the debris of a mask factory a brief argument which now figures in the sacred scriptures. That doctrinal work observed that the lottery is an interpolation of chance into the order of the world and that to accept errors is not to contradict chance: it is to corroborate it. It also observed that those lions and that sacred receptacle, although not disavowed by the Company (which did not renounce the right to consult them), function without official sanction (*F*, 71–72; *Lab.*, 33; *Fic.*, 68).

To get this passage in the right perspective, let us go back a moment to "The Library of Babel," where we were told that there were old men who hid themselves in the latrines with some metal disks in a prohibited dicebox (*F*, 9; *Lab.*, 56; *Fic.*, 84). Since metal disks or coins symbolize ideas or fictions, the figure here represents idealists (skeptics) imperfectly conceiving objective reality and juggling it about in their heads (conjecturing). This image follows, in "Babel," a description of a "blasphemous sect" that had suggested solving the riddle of the Universe (the Library) by juggling letters and symbols until the "right" combinations happened by accident. In Babylon the sacred latrine named Qaphqa is, like the privies of the Library, a place in which reality is subjectively conceived (fictionalized). Perhaps the quality of sacredness is ascribed to Kafka's work because it is as labyrinthine and unintelligible as the universe itself; it is an effective substitute for the world in its enigmatic, dream-like disorder, allowing the reader to bring the meaning to the form. It is indefinite, perhaps poly-valent—all things to all men, hence sacred by virtue of permitting subjective hypostatization.

This indefiniteness is also present in myths. Borges uses water and dust consistently to symbolize the primeval. A "dusty aque-duct" can be taken to refer to something primordial; but in an-other sense it is also an oxymoron, suggesting that which no longer conveys what it used to. A myth, like a dusty waterway, no longer conveys what it once did. "Cracks in a dusty aqueduct" perhaps means, if anything, "insights into ancient myths"; but more likely it implies the solution of ancient epistemological enigmas. "Stone lions" is obscure also. Stone is a Borgesian symbol for the funda-mental or primal, and lion is a hypostatic image that carries an overtone of the ancient and classic. By analogy with other figures, perhaps this phrase refers to substantial but imaginative tradition or literature, or to sacred scripture. It was believed, the story tells us, that these fissures and statues led to the Company—gave ac-cess to the ideational mechanism.

"People" (mental figments competing in the lottery) left in these places bits of information ("accusations," *delaciones*) that helped to inform the agents of the Company as to the intimate hopes and terrors (hopes of being and terrors of non-being) of the "popula-tion." To paraphrase again: it was believed that these were places where the attributes of the mental universe could commend them-selves to the attention of the consciousness, because these places —which are not "places" but are the containers of old and myth-ical concepts that imply a fantastic (non-conventional) ontology— supposedly have a direct appeal to the ideational mechanism or reveal something of it. "Persons" (attributes) either good or evil (useful or useless by conventional criteria) left in these receptacles their subjective complaints or petitions, which Borges character-izes as notices of variable veracity. I interpret: notices that *veracity is variable*.

These items are collected in an alphabetical file. Borges speaks of letters many times, as when Hladík found God in a tiny letter. Letters are to be associated with hypostatizing, and "alphabetical archive" may be taken to mean "file of letters," a collection of ideas, memories, impressions. A library or a mind (universe) can be called an alphabetical file in Borges' system.

"Incredibly, mutterings were not lacking. The Company, with its usual discretion, did not reply directly." The arbiter of knowledge, let us say, with its customary vagueness, would not be pinned down in the matter; or, the conceiving consciousness had no direct language to speak in. It preferred to scrawl its answer in "the debris of a mask factory." The words for "a mask factory"[4] suggest also "a making of masks" or "something which makes masks," and this immediately recalls "Everything and Nothing" (H, 43–45; Dream., 46–47), where Shakespeare and God both represent the play-acting, fictionmaking consciousness. "The debris of a mask factory" should be read "the aftermath of hypostatizing" with the suggestion that this aftermath is like the circular ruins and the ashes of the Phoenix; the consciousness scribbled its answer in the rubbish that had resulted from its conjecturing.

What was that answer, and what were the grumblings that provoked it? The citizen-attributes of Babylon were complaining that they did not win in the lottery; that is, they were not being hypostatized by the ideational machine. Each winner, or each drawing of the lottery, is a conjecture, a fiction of brief duration; and the people, each from his own point of view, were saying that the conjectures were not "correct." The Company replied that to accept error did not contradict chance—did not deny that the process was freely accidental—but corroborated it, for chance does not guarantee that every dog will have his day. The Company added that while it reserved the right to "consult" the "accusations" of the luckless attributes (their continual reminders that truth is variable), the vehicles of such complaints (the myths that exemplified

---

[4] "Una fábrica de caretas" is thus translated by John M. Fein in Labyrinths, p. 33, and by Anthony Kerrigan in Ficciones, p. 69.

the variability of truth) were not *guaranteed* to commend the un-
lucky, subordinate facets of reality to the attention of the consciousness. They "functioned without official sanction."

I suggest that the whole thing can be reduced to this: our truths
are, as Vaihinger said, nothing but useful errors—arbitrary fictions.
One may complain that other, even contradictory perspectives,
seemingly fantastic, are just as "true." The answer is this: to accept "error" as truth only corroborates the fact that the matter is
governed by "chance," the mind's subjective choice of what shall
be "true." As Vaihinger puts it, the objective untruth of a fiction is
the greatest proof of its usefulness to the consciousness, and therefore of its "truth" ('*As If*,' 32, 80, 94, 108, 168). Usefulness *is*
truth. What the Company does is right, for the Company is the
Company.

The rest of the story, both preceding and following the passage
cited above, is a repetition of a number of Borges' favorite ideas
regarding the compressibility of time and the justification of idealism as being the equivalent of objective reality. Borges invokes the
same theme that is generally present in "Examination of the Work
of Herbert Quain" and "The Garden of Forking Paths," which
amounts to the argument that one can have a succession of perspectives which exhausts all possibilities (if one is immortal!) and
that by having this succession telescoped into one moment we can
have, in effect, an Aleph: universal vision. How is this possible?
How can an infinite number of lottery drawings (hypostatizations)
coincide in time? Borges puts it thus:

The ignorant suppose that infinite drawings require an infinite time;
in reality it is enough that time be infinitely subdivisible, as the famous
parable of the contest with the tortoise shows. That infinitude agrees
in an admirable way with the sinuous numbers of Chance and with the
Celestial Archetype of the Lottery, which the Platonists worship (*F*,
73; *Lab.*, 34; *Fic.*, 70).

But the possession of all points of view and the simultaneous con-
sideration of all possible results of interrelated events does not

leave us with all of them; the Aleph is not a stable possession. On the contrary, what we have is the assurance that every particular thing, idea, or event has been selected, as if by an instantaneous IBM computer, from among all possibilities and assigned its moment of predominance. Time is held in some great reservoir, or *is* that reservoir, and it contains all variants. The incredible novel of Ts'ui Pên in "The Garden of Forking Paths" is the same labyrinth or universe as the Babylonian lottery. Of the Chinese author and his novel Borges says (in the words of the character Stephen Albert):

"Unlike Newton and Schopenhauer, your ancestor did not believe in a uniform and absolute time. He believed in infinite series of times, in a growing and vertiginous net of divergent, convergent, and parallel times. That network of times which approach each other, fork, stop short, or are unaware of each other for centuries, embraces *all* possibilities. We do not exist in most of those times; in some you exist and not I; in others, I, not you; in others, both of us" (*F*, 109–110; *Lab*., 28; *Fic*., 100).

Even in such abstruse sophistry as this, which is so typical of Borges, we are dealing with the Zahir (path, *sendero*) and with the Aleph or the simultaneous aggregation of all paths. The Zahir is, for Borges, the truth of "the realist, who longs for . . . the tranquil archetypes of things," and the Aleph is the truth of the "nominalist, who denies the truth of the archetypes and wants to congregate in a second the details of the universe" (*HE*, 34).

"Forking Paths" and "Herbert Quain"

Having spoken of the simultaneous congregation of the details of the universe, we have substantially summed up "The Garden of Forking Paths" and "Examination of the Work of Herbert Quain" with regard to the manner in which they reflect the motif. In the former, the literary labyrinth of Ts'ui Pên contains all the possible cross-arrangements of time and its contents, conceived nonetheless as if unfolding linearly and running in some vague direction. In "Quain," however, the direction is reversed. Instead of conceiving, for example, an event with all of its possible consequences, Quain's literary work conceives a consequence and moves back to all of its possible causes. The details of these schemes are not relevant here; in both stories we are again shown the conceptual contrast between an object, or a point in space or time, as representative of the universe (in other words, a Zahir) and, on the other hand, an object or point which *is* the universe by virtue of its ability to contain all other objects and points, like the Aleph. This sophistry, as presented in "Quain," is not represented as action or clouded over with intriguing metaphors that lend an air of fantasy or archetypal reality. The usual symbols of Zahir and Aleph are therefore almost altogether lacking.

"The Garden of Forking Paths" is a more interesting story, but it requires little further comment. The usual symbols appear; the uses of some of these have been mentioned already. Early in the story we can assume that someone is going to be killed, for the protagonist is accompanied by a mention of a quadrangular coin— a faded or fading reality. However, the image here seems also to indicate that the man who will do the killing, Yu Tsun, is not sufficiently "real" or powerful to make his voice heard in Germany, where the Luftwaffe awaits the information he wants to send. His chief in Germany is, let us say, the consciousness in which an idea must be hypostatized before the story is finished. Yu Tsun has to find a way of conveying to him the name of an English city named Albert. Yu Tsun goes to the home of Stephen Albert, who lives appropriately in *Ashgrove,* another oxymoron composed of ash and trees and having about the same value as the quadrangular coin. Against the background of the garden and the labyrinthine novel, both of which are symbols of the universal chaos, Yu Tsun shoots Albert, and the report of the murder of this prominent man will reach Germany. The omission of the word *time* from Ts'ui Pên's novel is said in the story to be the key to its identity as a time-puzzle; and the "omission" of Stephen Albert is a hypostatization of the city which bears his name. Thus the theme of the story—the bifurcation of time and destiny—is only the instrument of the motif, which is semantic. Symbolism of the French school and the "esthetic reality" are again suggested.

"Funes the Memorious"

Let us go back for a moment to the miserable Funes. There are enlightening details yet to be mentioned in his regard. The reason for his paralysis is the same as that of Recabarren: his inability to reduce reality to the form of single hypostatizations. He lies in darkness and hardly sleeps. Borges tosses in a handful of images to symbolize his condition of universality: his face is Indian-like, his maté cup bears the arms of the Banda Oriental (East Bank, i.e., Uruguay), and a yellow mat is placed over his window.

We first see Funes when Borges and his cousin Bernardo Haedo are riding *horseback*. A *storm* the color of a blackboard comes up and *obscures the sun*, the *trees go crazy*, and Borges wants to run before they are caught by the "elemental *water*." They take shelter between two elevated brick *paths* or sidewalks and Borges sees Funes running along one of these paths as if along a *wall*. Paths are hypostatic symbols and walls stand for the mythic or universal; but both these images are modified, the path being not quite a path and rather like a wall that is "narrow and broken." Funes is given the character, in other words, of both Zahir and Aleph. Indeed, at this juncture he is mentally normal except that he already has indications of a kind of Alephosis. He remembers names phenomenally, and he is able to tell the exact hour without consulting the sky. Funes later contrasts his "memorious" condition with what he was before the accident that changed him:

. . . before that rainy afternoon when the roof-tile bowled him over, he had been what every human being is: blind, deaf, harebrained, forgetful (*F*, 122; *Lab.*, 63; *Fic.*, 112).

Like all men, he was at that time able to forget details. But not any more; now he can reconstruct the last detail of a whole day, and it takes him a whole day to do it. Not only can he remember absolutely every event, but he can visualize anything in the most microscopic and vivid detail, and these intensely particular items are enumerated in deftly-modified symbols that show the universe as a collection of tiny, repetitive units or successive and singular moments:

. . . the disordered mane of a colt . . . a herd of cattle on a hill . . . the changing fire . . . the innumerable ashes . . . the many faces of a dead man during a long wake (*F*, 123–124; *Lab.*, 64; *Fic.* 112).

Poor Funes is neither Aleph nor Zahir; his mind is a duplicate of the universe, a horrible proliferation of endless particulars, but bound in linear time. If it could all be present in one moment he would be an Aleph, or a mystic. But lacking simultaneity, he is only a congestion. This is the problem presented in the story: the vision of the whole universe must not occur unless time is stopped. The Aleph is finally impossible, and the nominalist must ultimately perish of "pulmonary congestion."

"The Writing of the God"

The question of time and of mysticism brings us to the unforgettable experience of Tzinacán. In my opinion this is one of Borges' very best stories. I said earlier that Tzinacán's mystical experience ought to be thought of as a return to the mythic ground of being, a kind of pantheism. This is only to say that it is not any particular God with whom Tzinacán is joined, but with Being, the universe. There is also a mysticism of the Zahir, and this is precisely what Tzinacán is striving to experience until he gives up and is united with, let us say, the God who transcends theism. Just as Droctulft the Lombard is "loyal to captain and tribe, but not to the universe" until he sees the magnificent, labyrinthine city, and just as Otto zur Linde cries before the god of violence, "Let heaven be, though our place be in hell," Tzinacán's real objective is to vindicate the god of the pyramid, of whom he is the last remaining priest. The mystical or mythic experience comes only after he has abandoned all gods who are less than the universe in size, which means that he has abandoned hope. Hope exists only as a Zahir.

Tzinacán is the last priest of the god who wrote, in the beginning of time, a secret formula in an unknown place for the last man to read. The writing can restore the sacred pyramid, free the prisoner Tzinacán, make him omnipotent and immortal, and enable him to take revenge on his tormentor, Pedro de Alvarado. After countless years in the total darkness of his semicircular stone cell, the Aztec comes to the conclusion that the writing can only have been recorded as a configuration of markings on the skin of a tiger. A wall divides the cell, and beyond it paces a jaguar.[5] To paraphrase, the formula for omnipotence, as in "The Lottery in Babylon," can exist only in and as the configuration of the hypostatizing mind: only in the structure of knowledge that the mind builds and of which the mind consists. But what is the crowning knowledge, the ultimate creation, to which the mind comes? It is the understanding of itself as a mind that has created itself by creating its own "reality"—a mind that has no objective knowledge and therefore has no objective existence. The final knowledge, the ultimate fiction, is that a man is only an illusion.

Tzinacán lies in total darkness, but at high noon he is able to hypostatize the universe (to behold a Zahir that implies the universe):

At the shadowless hour [noon], a trapdoor opens in the ceiling and a jailer whom the years have been erasing works an iron pulley and lowers to us, at the end of a rope, jars of water and chunks of meat. The light enters the dome; at that instant I can see the tiger (A, 115).

[5] *Tigre* is a popular synonym for *jaguar* in Spanish America. In other stories Borges writes of tigers, having in mind the Asian type. Cf. "The Zahir," where there are Himalayan tigers on the walls of the jail in Nittur (A, 111; *Lab.*, 162).

Midday, light, instant, tiger—all against a background of round-
ness, stone, darkness, a wall.[6]

The jaguar is "an attribute of the god," like all hypostatized
things existing in a hierarchy, and implies an infinity of others:

I considered that even in human languages there is no proposition that
does not imply the whole universe; to say *tiger* is to say the tigers that
engendered him, the deer and tortoises he ate, the grass that nourished
the deer, the earth that was the mother of the grass, the sky that gave
light to the earth (*A*, 118).

Tzinacán's whole system of thought, and his mental struggle to
discern the god-writing and the meaning of the implied universe,
is composed of this kind of hypostatization. It is a mental structure
made of parts that imply wholes, culminating in a supreme hypostat, the secret formula, which will justify an intellectual pyramid.
   Tzinacán is, in other words, a man to whom the word and the
thing are equal. In every moment he is "loyal" like Droctulft to one
aspect of reality, forgetting the connotations. He has built his
structure of knowledge upon mere partial aspects of what he himself is: he is an avenger, a decipherer of a mystery, and a priest of
the god. He begins to think. He "dreams" of a grain of sand (he
hypostatizes one of the infinite particles of reality) and wakes up
(accepts that particle as objectively real). He sleeps again, dreaming that there are two grains, and awakens. A third time he dreams,
there are three grains, and he wakes. Finally the grains fill the cell
and he is dying under a hemisphere of sand. He realizes that he is
dreaming, not knowing, and he makes a great effort to "wake up"

   [6] With regard to the tiger as the symbol of both Zahir and universe-as-
Zahir, compare "The Zahir" where Borges describes the "infinite tiger" painted
in the jail of Nittur, made up of innumerable tigers and tigers-within-tigers—
infinite hypostatizations, which if they could be simultaneous would comprise
the Aleph. Borges' other references to tigers are many, the most noteworthy
being "The Other Tiger" (*H*, 75; *Dream.*, 70), in which he describes the
symbolic tiger and the real one, and then the inexpressible ideal tiger he
searches for, which will live only in the moment, without past or future, and
will be a system of words and "a form of my dream."

in the sense of to reach the top of the pyramid, to win the struggle for total comprehension—to have the magic formula. But when he is most wakeful the sand still suffocates him. "Someone" says to him:

You have not waked up to reality, but to a former dream. That dream is within another dream, and so on to infinity, which is the number of the grains of sand. The road which you are to unwalk is interminable and you will die before you have truly wakened (A, 119).

Let me clarify the basic idea involved here and in what follows. In the mind of the idealist and the mythic thinker, when one thing is equivalent to another it "kills" it; it becomes it. As the Symbolist puts it, a word kills an idea by taking its place. Tzinacán realizes that in each of his dreams he equates himself with the contents of his dream; and recognizing this, he shouts in rebellion or repentance: "A dream-sand cannot kill me and there are no dreams within dreams!" A mountain of sand in his mind, of his own creation, cannot kill him—cannot be equivalent to him, cannot account for him—and there are no (read *there shall be no*) hypostatizations built upon others, no piling up of falsities. Now fully conscious of the nature of his "knowledge" and the error of perspectivizing, Tzinacán understands that the route of passage from one perspective to another must lie across the primordial ground of the equality of substance. From one point of view he is a priest; from another, a decipherer of the secret; from another, an avenger. But these cannot be placed one upon the other; the latter cannot presuppose the former. They must stand side by side on the same ground, and even then the ground itself has something more to offer to his understanding: there is something fundamental to which he finally is equivalent. He is a prisoner in a semicircular cell, a mere attribute of the god, another of the countless objects of the universe.

A man assumes, gradually, the form of his destiny; a man is, in the long run, his circumstances. More than a decipherer or an avenger, more than a priest of the god, I was a prisoner (A, 119).

Now he is truly awake, having been awakened by the brilliance in the top of the dome. The brightness of day streams down upon him out of a "circle of light." This mixed image signifies that Tzinacán's knowledge is an utter paradox: no-knowledge is the ultimate knowledge. The mythic formlessness (the circle) is also the light into which all things vanish, and the end is the same as the beginning.

Tzinacán blesses his circumstances; he blesses the primeval mud, so to speak, of myth. But he also blesses the implied union of Zahir and Aleph, he blesses the hopelessness of the skeptic. He puts his benediction upon the most elemental symbols of the idealist's universe and mode of knowledge:

From the endless labyrinth of dreams I came back to my hard prison as if I were coming home. I blessed its humidity, I blessed its tiger, I blessed its hole of light, I blessed my old and aching body, I blessed the darkness and the rock (A, 119).

He then testifies that there are two kinds of "union with the divinity," two kinds of mystical experience; but he does not know whether they are finally two or one: the universal (mythic) vision which he achieved, and the mystical Zahir-vision which substitutes for it. And how, indeed, can he know this, since the fiction of no-fiction is itself a fiction? He says:

Then there occurred a union with the divinity, with the universe (I do not know if these words differ). Ecstasy does not repeat its symbols; there are some who have seen God in a great light, there are those who have perceived him in a sword or in the circles of a rose (A, 120).

"A great light" (*un resplandor*) is a strong Zahir symbol, as is the sword. The rose is, too; but here it is modified by "circles." The latter image calls to mind the Runic cross, while the idea of being united with God through a dogmatic hypostatization suggests orthodox religion and recalls "The Cult of the Phoenix," in which honor is accorded those who dispense with the Secret (provisional or conjectural hypostatizing) and obtain direct union with the divinity; that is, orthodox religious mystics, non-skeptical believers.[7] But Tzinacán saw no Zahir; he saw a giant wheel that was everywhere at once, made of water but also of fire (made of objective reality but also of subjective interpretation), and infinite.[8] The Aztec priest's final victory, his final knowledge, is philosophical idealism. He has seen everything, including the "faceless god who is behind the gods." He now sees infinite processes that form a single "happiness." He has found the secret of the functioning of his own mind; he knows the form of its activity; and the joy of understanding, he says, is greater than that of imagining or feeling.

Now he understands, moreover, the writing of the god. The inscription consists of forty syllables, fourteen words. Borges uses these numbers in their conventional acceptation as symbols of indefiniteness, polyvalence, or infinity. Tzinacán will not pronounce the formula, he says, because he has forgotten himself; he has become nothing. The infinite words of the formula are the same thing as the mountain of sand, and he will not pronounce them— he will dream no more—because he and his consciousness are illusions.

Critics here and there, possibly taking their cue from Barrenechea, have fixed Tzinacán's loss of self under the heading of nihilism. Barrenechea says (*Irrealidad*, pp. 87–88; *Borges the Labyrinth*

---

[7] This obscure statement can be taken in the opposite sense also: honor is accorded those who dispense with the making of any kind of "god," even a provisional one, and obtain a pantheistic union with Being. This interpretation would tend to indicate a sharp division in Borges' mind between idealism and the pantheism usually attributed to him in this story.

[8] Compare Alan Watts, *Myth and Ritual in Christianity*, p. 29 n.: "It is a universal feature of the *philosophia perennis* that what we experience as the succession of time is an abstraction rather than a reality, and that the real state of the universe is eternal or timeless—a 'moment' without past or future." And p. 99, where Watts equates the scriptural " 'strait and narrow gate' or 'needle's eye' " with the "timeless, eternal moment wherein our real life consists." In a footnote, p. 99, he adds: "The 'point' is the *bindu* of the Hindu tradition, or the *ekaksana*, the 'one moment' of the Buddhist, which is the same as Dante's *punto a cui tutti li tempi son presenti . . .* in *Paradiso*, xvii."

Maker, p. 89) that Borges ends "The Writing of the God" by plunging the protagonist from the heights of ecstasy to an absolute nothing. She associates the ecstasy with Tzinacán's "participation in God and the universe" as if this were a separate and contrastive state preceding his self-loss, and the implication is that the priest's final state is some kind of misery. I think there is a subtle error here that grows with elaboration. Tzinacán is not plunged from a pinnacle of ecstasy to an absolute nothing. He becomes reconciled to his prison and blesses it precisely because of the ecstatic revelation, although he had previously been convinced that he could escape his prison by pronouncing the formula; and this should remind us of Asterion, who denied that his open-doored prison was really a prison. We may also remember the jailbirds of Babylon, who went to prison to *avoid* becoming nothing. Tzinacán the prisoner loses only his delusion that he, an attribute of the universe, should be a hypostat, a universe in himself. He loses, I grant, his identity as a self-contained individual and becomes "nobody," which shows that the Zahirist or god-worshipper and the closed-door solipsist are the same thing—but he is neither. Tzinacán retains his participation in the universe as one who accedes to an objective reality which he can know, and has known, only subjectively. He has become nothing only in the sense that he is now "loyal to the universe." This is not a negative nihilism, not the self-eradication of the Buddhist; it is like Vaihinger's "positivist idealism," which consists in the courageous idea that one's self is not ultimate. Asterion is lonely, but he is not finally alone. He can go out of his house at any time. Again a paradox: one can be a mere attribute of the universe, a creature of the Creator, only by realizing and accepting one's "omnipotence." Tzinacán's final state is blessed. He can rebuild his mountain of sand, he can pronounce his magic formula; but he will never do it because it constitutes infinite self-delusion, "salvation," intellectual death. Unlike Asterion, Tzinacán scorns the "redeemer."

"The Immortal"

In this story Borges has made a very simple equation or parallel. An immortal being is a dogma; a mortal being is a provisional hypostatization, one that can die in the sense of becoming, like the jail inmates of Babylon, a connotation or submerged aspect. As Homer and the narrator of the story show, mortality is finally preferable to indestructibility. The mortality of ideas, or of perceptions in the sense of momentary arrangements of reality, is the basic characteristic of the idealist mind. For Borges, consequently, the idealist intellect is the true reflection of the mind of God, in which *men* are ideas and the form of provisional hypostatization is the form of life itself: God "thinks" a man, and when he ceases to think him, he disappears. An immortal man is inconsistent with the omnipotence of God, and a dogma is inconsistent with the omnipotence that Borges ascribes to the Company in Babylon. In "The Lottery in Babylon" the Company represents a faculty that determines "knowledge"; it can form it and remove it. Borges is unable to put his finger on this entity, and for that reason he ends the story with speculation about whether the Company exists and what it consists of.

A quotation from Francis Bacon sets the theme of "The Immortal":

Salomon saith. *There is no new thing upon the earth.* So that as Plato had an imagination, *that all knowledge was but remembrance;* so Salomon giveth his sentence, *that all novelty is but oblivion.*

Francis Bacon: Essays, LVIII.

To paraphrase again, Plato said that all knowledge is but the preservation or recall of a hypostatization, and Solomon said that all new things are only Babylonian captives set free and hypostatized.

According to his usual but not invariable way, Borges here treats men (God's ideas) as if they were ideas in the human mind; he substitutes human immortality for the deathlessness of an idea or world view. Much is added to the story to embellish it and to show the ramifications of the simple equation.

Joseph Cartaphilus has gray eyes, a gray beard, and "singularly vague features." Immediately we know that Cartaphilus is on his way out of existence; he is dying, or will die. Within the next two sentences he has done so. Perishing at sea, he leaves a manuscript which comprises the tale.

In the beginning he was a Roman tribune named Marco (Mark: German coin) Flaminio (Flaminian Way: road) Rufo (redhead). Hope or ambition is what causes "men" to seek hypostatization, and Rufo and his followers sought *glory* near the *Red* Sea. There is general disappointment when glory is not achieved: many who "magnanimously coveted the steel" (who ambitiously coveted full-ness of being) were consumed by *fever* and *magic* (were never able to ex-ist, to stand out). The tribune's disappointment over his obscurity made him resolve to find the City of the Immortals—to find, that is, his own elevation to immutable full-being.

Once hypostatization is established as the goal, Borges rains its symbols upon the reader. In six short lines we find the following: the narrator's search begins in a *garden* (in mythic formlessness); all that *night* he did not *sleep*, but he *got up* a little before *dawn*, when all hypostatizing begins; his slaves (his connotations) did not; in the background of these actions the *moon* had the same color as the *sand*. A *tired horseman* (dying hypostat), who was *bloody* (was losing his reality), came out of the east. The horseman *falls off* his horse and dies a little before *dawn*. Dawn is the dreaming time, when the mind arbitrarily disarranges reality. The horseman's *blood* was *dark*—another oxymoron, here indicating im-permanent or modified existence. The rider was looking for the City of the Immortals, we are told.

A number of the images that follow seem to exist only for the sake of multiplying symbols; they are incidental to the narrator's travels. A hypostat symbol is "the mountain that gave a name to the ocean" (*A*, 9; *Lab.*, 107). Some men sleep with their faces exposed to the moon; they are called rash, as if their exposure to this symbol of universality were an unnecessary risk of losing "glory." There is a neat combination here of Borgesian symbol with the conventional idea of being moon-struck: these "reckless ones" become feverish. Other men drink water that drives them mad. Contact with the moon and with water causes these "men" to lose their chance of being hypostatized in the ideal universe, although they come near it (the use of "fever" indicates this). This imagery prefigures the experience of Rufo, who becomes immortal only by being absorbed into the universal madness or chaos.

The sun, symbol of fiction and at times of dogma, is used here to foretell the undesirability of the immortality which the narrator is to achieve. In all his travels there is repeated mention of the terrible overhead sun that dehydrates the men and fills the narrator with thirst and the fear of thirst. A deftly-executed symbolism that not only fits perfectly into the literal or real-life context but also into the private imagery of the motif, and that foreshadows the narrator's longing to return to a mortal state, is his hallucination, on horseback and under the sun, that he is trying to reach a jar of water (*A*, 10; *Lab.*, 107).

This image suggests that the nearer he approaches to the City of the Immortals the more real or more nearly immortal he becomes. The hallucination of the water jar occurs within sight of the *pyramids* and *towers* of the city. Also, as he has drawn nearer he has been shedding his attributes. He had many soldiers and slaves, but he arrives at the city alone. The followers were lost through desertion and mutiny. The mutineers represent an attack on his increasingly dogmatic existence, and to overcome these rivals he acts as a hypostat should: "I proceeded straight." He finally has to flee the mutineers with the few soldiers who remain faithful, and he loses these under the correct symbolic circumstances: "In the desert I lost them, among the spirals of sand and the vast night" (*A*, 10; *Lab.*, 107). Now he is alone, an elemental reality of only one aspect, an irreducible being—an immutable (if "God" wills) Zahir.

There is a point somewhere at which a Zahir becomes, or substitutes for, the Aleph; or rather, it seems to do so when it becomes canonized as truth. With his habitual subtlety and precision, Borges at this juncture makes a total shift of symbolism from Zahir to Aleph, for this reason: a dogma is an illusion that does not know it is illusory; it is an ideality turned objective and negotiable; hence, when it comes into being as a rigid Zahir that thinks it is an Aleph, it may assume the qualities of the universal. When Rufo the tribune finds the immortals, they are gray men with unkempt beards, and naked.

Also, they have lost the power of speech. Language is the concomitant of the Zahir, not of the ambiguous or the chaotic. The immortals, who are Troglodytes, fulfill Borges' dictum that an immortal man is all men (A, 21; Lab., 115); he sees all, knows all, is all. A mental reality that equates to the universe cannot be spoken except as a single word, as Borges tells us in "The Writing of the God" (A, 118). To speak that word would fulminate the thing it represents. Schiller said that knowledge is death; the Troglodytes are like walking dead men who feel no joy or sorrow and hardly even see.

Having drunk from the river that confers immortality, the narrator lies outside the city as if between life and death: "Naked on the unknown sand, I let the moon and the sun play with my sad destiny." Both the sun and the moon are victorious in this contest, for they have somehow become one. Death is immortality, and immortality is death; the Zahir is the Aleph; to be is to be all things, and to be all things is to be no *one* thing. Absolute being is absolute nonbeing. All of which is to say that man lives only so long as he is mortal and singular—only so long as he knows the ups and downs, the recurring lives and deaths, of a provisional figment in a Mind. The members of the sacerdotal college of Babylon, who entered into the lottery more fervently than the envious poor people, "enjoyed all the vicissitudes of terror and hope," and the poor resented their own exclusion from "that rhythm, notoriously delicious" (F, 70; Lab., 32; Fic., 67).

The description of the unconscionable City of the Immortals is not relevant here. The men cursed with immortality had built a wild insanity of brick and stone, horrible to look at. The symbols of hypostatization disappear for a while, to reappear when Rufo and the Troglodyte (who is Homer) begin to desire mortality. Absolute knowledge is madness and meaninglessness, and they want to return to the relative, momentary, and self-justified "knowledge" of finite man. Borges brings in again the question of memory and forgetfulness, analogous to immortality and its opposite; this reminds us of Funes and of the language of Tlön, which has infinite adjectives from which nouns have to be hypostatized. Borges compares such a language to the mind of the immortal Homer:

It occurred to me that perhaps there were no objects for him, but a vertiginous and continual play of very brief impressions. I thought of a world without memory, without time; I considered the possibility of a language in which nouns would be unknown (A, 17; Lab., 112).

Homer, like Funes and Recabarren, cannot hypostatize single things; he cannot focus his attention upon one and ignore others. For this reason he cannot speak; he sees the universe in detail.

Now the symbols of life begin to return. The country of the immortals is almost waterless, ruled by the pitiless sun. The nights on the desert are usually cold, but one occurs that seems "a fire." Something, we know, is going to change; fire is about to consume objectivity. Rufo, who had dreamed of water before reaching the city, now dreams of a river "coming to rescue me." It rains on the red sand and the black rock. Rufo receives it naked, like the rest; they receive it as the night "declines" under the yellow clouds. The immortals are like frenzied priests of a god; Homer whimpers and regains his speech.

To shorten Borges' longest story, Rufo and Homer go in search of the river that will make them mortal again. We lose sight of Homer, but Rufo finds the river after centuries. Climbing up the bank after routinely tasting its waters, he scratches his hand on a tree, feels pain, and sees the symbol of his return to the life of a happy and provisional hypostat: blood.

The rest of the story involves us again in the equation of all men with one man. Rufo is somehow Homer as well as Cartaphilus. Surely this is a repetition, not of Borges' seeming insistence that all men are literally one man, but of the belief that all ideal perspectives of reality are but the same reality variously viewed: the faces, or the ninety-nine names, of God. "Perhaps the history of the universe is the history of a few metaphors" (*OI*, 13; *Oth. Inq.*, 9).

"The Wait"

"The Wait" seems to be, but is not, a simple case of hypostatic rivalry like "The End." It is richer, more imaginative. The stranger who arrives at the boarding house is a less-than-something who has become an entity by force of hope or will, and his something-thingness is in question. He has fled from his Gestalt, where he did not always predominate, and he is hiding where he does not belong in order to preserve his independence from fellow attributes with whom he was forced to compete as if in a Babylonian lottery. He is an egregious being who wants to go on existing as such, but at the same time he does not like the insecurity of his hypostatization.

The enemy who is hunting him down is not a rival being, but Being itself, the whole conjunct of reality from which he has fled. It is not merely the enmity of the man Villari that he has incurred, but a kind of cosmic hostility that causes him to seek a paradoxical obscurity. The thing he is waiting for is not the inevitable encounter with Villari; he is waiting for things to "settle down." Villari is not a man, but somehow is the representative of all the attributes that were deserted when the protagonist (who, appropriately, has no name of his own) left their company. The stranger takes the name of Villari, his enemy, because when they ask him his name he is "unable to think of any other." The real Villari is the spokesman, so to speak, for the family the stranger has left, and the stranger makes good his escape every night in his dreams by shooting Villari and the two men who accompany him.

As the story begins, a man arrives by car one morning to take a room at a house. The number of the house is four thousand and four; a rather square or symmetrical number, we might say. There are square plots of ground around the trees in front, and opposite the sidewalk in front of the house is the long, windowless wall of a hospital. The sun, we notice here, is not shining from the sky but is "reverberating, at a distance, on some greenhouses."

The man looks at these surroundings and finds them to be "arbitrary and casual and in whatever order, like those that are seen in dreams," and he hopes that in time, if God wills, they will be "invariable, necessary, and familiar." He hopes, let us say, that in time the Gestalt into which he has fled will become fixed and accepted.[9] He notices that the name on the pharmacy nearby is Breslauer; the Jews are replacing the Italians in the vicinity, who had replaced the Creoles. This was good; he preferred "not to alternate with people of his own blood" (A, 137; Lab., 165); that is, he preferred not to be alternately dominant and subordinate with the entities who, along with him, comprised his "blood," his being.

To symbolize further the idea that the man wants not to be noticed in his new "country," Borges gives us the incident of the coins. The man pays the cab driver and unintentionally gives him a foreign twenty-centavo coin, which the driver returns. Embar-

---

[9] Analogously, this can be taken as an expression of the hope that idealism will become the philosophy of men. The symbolic elements appearing in this description of the surroundings represent things hypostatized upon the substratum of mythic formlessness or equality: trees standing in square plots; sidewalk (path) beside a wall, et cetera. This undertanding of "truth," the narrator hopes, will become invariable, necessary, familiar.

rassed, the stranger gives him forty centavos. Then he says to himself: "I am obligated to act in such a way that everybody will forget me. I have committed two errors: I have given a coin from another country and I have let it be seen that that mistake is important to me" (A, 138; *Lab.*, 165). The foreign coin symbolizes his status as a fugitive being, an alien.

The stranger is installed in a room containing some of the typical symbols: red walls, an iron bedstead decorated with branches and tendrils (reminiscent of forking paths and bifurcating destinies); and the figures on the wallpaper are peacocks, symbolic of pride. When the landlady asks him his name he replies "Villari,"

. . . not as a secret defiance, not to mitigate a humiliation which, in truth, he did not feel, but because that name troubled him and it was impossible for him to think of any other (A, 138; *Lab.*, 166).

It was not possible for him to think of another name because, as a being who had abandoned his "family," he had no name of his own. Villari was the name of his village, his *villar*,[10] which he had betrayed. The humiliation that Borges says the protagonist did not feel "in truth" is possibly the abasement which he did not feel in his other conjunct. Perhaps he is a dominant feature of reality who wanted to lose his appended attributes in the Gestalt called Villari because of the constant threat or necessity of having to "alternate" with them. He wants to be rid of the village, of Villari, once and for all. Installed in his red room, he waits for news that the composite entity called Villari has died (A, 139; *Lab.*, 166–167).

Because the attributes in the Villari group bear the name collectively, the Villari who is killed and the Villari who kills him are in a sense the same man. Borges shows us this: in his dreams, the stranger is repeatedly hunted down by Villari and two other men, presumably because this is the total number of men comprising the ideal group. But when Villari finally comes, he is accompanied by

[10] Remember Teodelina Villar, whose name seems to suggest "little goddess of a village."

only one. The third man is the stranger himself. When he has died, just beyond the last words of the story, he will no doubt walk away with Villari and the other and the three of them will be "Villari." He will have returned to where he belongs, a condition in which he alternates with men of his own blood.

Further indication of this is given in the stranger's attitude toward art. Going back to Borges' concept of art as mythical or imaginative thought, of which the alternation of attributes is the essential feature, we can see that the stranger identifies himself only with conventional reality, not with anything imaginative or fantastic. When he goes to the movies he never sits close to the screen. We are told:

. . . the idea of a coincidence between art and reality was alien to him . . . he never saw himself as a personage of art (A, 139; *Lab.*, 166).

He never saw himself as art; but, we learn later, he does try in a docile way to like the unrealities he sees on the screen. Secretly he wants to like them, we suspect; secretly he knows he belongs with them, and he longs for them. He would feel some measure of relief if he were with his fellows again. This is why he reacts with anger, but also with a measure of relief, when he is pushed in a crowd by a tall young man accompanied by a German-looking woman (A, 140; *Lab.*, 167), who he fears may have recognized him.

The movies he sees are about the criminal underworld, or to say it more patently, the jailbirds, the underlings:

He saw tragic stories of the underworld; these no doubt included errors; these no doubt included images that were also images of his former life (A, 139; *Lab.*, 166).

He was himself one of those underlings, but his "powerful will . . . had moved the hatred of men" (A, 139; *Lab.*, 167). He has spent years in solitude, for he has had other "reclusions" before this one (A, 139; *Lab.*, 166). He has been trying for a long time to get away. Now he wants only to "endure; not conclude." He tries to live in the mere present, without memories or anticipations, like the old dog that lives in the rooming house.

Meditating, the stranger does not believe that Dante would consign him to the last circle (the circle of traitors), where Ugolino's teeth endlessly gnaw Ruggieri's neck. This gives us the key to the title of the story and testifies further to the repeated symbolism of the jail. The Ugolino of history was betrayed by Ruggieri and thrown into prison, along with relatives, and there they all starved to death after reportedly turning to cannibalism. Here the stranger has thrown "Villari" into an ideal limbo and is waiting for the death of the villagers. This connection with the ugly history of Ugolino is exploited in another paragraph of the story, where the stranger suffers a toothache that is called a "horrible miracle" and the extraction of the tooth is termed a crisis or peril (*trance*).

Much more could be said, but this is enough. The real Villari finally comes, early one morning, to kill the stranger. His death occurs in the morning rather than at evening, no doubt, because it is not a real death but the reintegration of the reality "Villari." Another man is with Villari. The stranger motions for them to wait, and turns his *face* to the *wall*: he turns his egregious being in the direction of the universal chaos, back toward that condition of alternating reality from which he had escaped. Borges asks: Was it to gain their pity? Was it because it was easier to accept his fate than to be forever awaiting it? Or was it in order that the killers might be a dream, as they had been so many times in the same place and at the same hour?

The third possibility is the right one, if we look at it from the standpoint of the veiled language. The protagonist surrendered his separate being in order that the three men might again be a "dream," a conjunct, an ideal reality made up of substance and attributes forever alternating. The idea that this has occurred before in the same place and time, besides being consistent with the real-life situation in the story, suggests one of Borges' favorite sophisms, that time is a static reservoir and that the past, present, and future are all occurring now and forever.

There are indications in the story that the stranger half hopes that Villari will come; he somehow resembles Asterion waiting hopefully for his deadly redeemer.

"Emma Zunz"

To kill Loewenthal with "justice" Emma Zunz has to become a metaphor for her father. "Justice" means idealist rationality. In real life there is nothing irrational about Emma's taking revenge in her own name and right upon the man who stole money and caused her father to be accused and exiled and finally to commit suicide. But Emma is an attribute in the mental universe and must follow the rules of orderly mental procedure. No other story by Borges lays so much stress on "la Justicia de Dios," and no other mentions justice by that name more often (*A*, 61, 63, twice on 64; *Lab.*, 134, 135, 136). The justice of God is, in this story, the proper alignment of conceptual forms, or simply the laws of rhetoric.

In a real-life manner of speaking, Emma has to kill Loewenthal in her father's name, not her own; otherwise her deed will be murder rather than justice. Borges tells us that it is not out of fear but because she is a tool of justice that she does not want to be punished (*A*, 64; *Lab.*, 136). It would be "unjust" (irrational, logically incorrect) if she were jailed or obliterated for eliminating Loewenthal, not *for* her father, but *as* her father; such a thing would be tantamount to a loss of substance or the disappearance of a form from the ideal universe.

Let us look at it this way: Loewenthal is a hypostat, and so is Emmanuel Zunz.[11] Emma is an attribute of her father. Loewenthal has displaced Zunz in a traitorous manner; that is, in the ideal scheme the Loewenthal reality has been unjustly substituted for

[11] "Emmanuel" may have been chosen for its meaning of "God with us." Zunz is indeed "with us" in his daughter, and her name is a diminutive of his.

the Zunz reality, and "justice" (perhaps Vaihinger's "usefulness") calls for the reestablishment of Zunz. But "revenge" can be taken only by Zunz himself, not by his attribute Emma, for an ideal *res* cannot be displaced by the mere adjectival characteristic of another *res*. Zunz is dead. His Gestalt is a hierarchy without a crown, an entity without a name, a pregnant situation. The only way the mind can handle it is to call it, metonymically, by one of its attributes. Emma must stand proxy for her father. But she cannot be hypostatized as a *res* in her own right, because she is not the same reality as her father. The Emmanuel-Emma corporeity is necessary, but it is doomed to remain an ambiguous, meta-phorical, esthetic reality even after it has avenged itself on the usurper Loewenthal.

In order to substitute for her father and act in his name, Emma must assume his essence—that of a wronged hypostat. It does not matter that the one who wrongs her is not Loewenthal, or that she herself invites the injury.[12]

The story is primarily one about form and matter, as Borges seems to declare at the end. After killing Loewenthal, Emma tele-phones the police and says: "An unbelievable thing has happened. . . . Mr. Loewenthal sent for me, using the strike as a pretext. . . . He took advantage of me, I killed him . . ." (*A*, 65; *Lab.*, 137). It is indeed "unbelievable" because the facts are other than those implied; but as Borges says, the words are substantially true: "True was the manner of Emma Zunz, true the modesty, true the hatred. True also was the outrage she had suffered; only the cir-

---

[12] This is true because Borges apparently understands concepts or ideas to be constant in number (originality or creativity is impossible). In the ideal economy there are somehow more ideas than the consciousness can use. "Justice," or in this case revenge, is not achieved merely by restoring Zunz, but by simultaneously eliminating Loewenthal. Being wronged is merely a technical matter of being humiliated by an equal; Loewenthal is not Emma's equal, but her superior, until she assumes her father's form. The sailor who is the "instrument of divine justice" has no name and she is careful not to learn his name; he is her fellow nonentity, her equal in the hierarchy of ideal being.

cumstances, the hour, and one or two proper names were false" (*A*, 66; *Lab.*, 137).

This gives the impression that the action is taking place above the world in an archetypal realm. But on the contrary, we see in "Emma Zunz" the same downward regression to myth that we find in every instance where a change of reality occurs. When Emma goes to find a sailor by whom she can be properly outraged, the episode is described as a "brief chaos" (*A*, 62; *Lab.*, 134), and its narration begins with the usual array of hypostatic symbols mixed with those of the mythic substructure. The always-exact Borges is conscious that he is presenting not the displacement of one hypostat by another, but the illegitimate or expedient movement of a mere attribute from a subordinate to a dominant position. This makes it difficult to visualize whether an attribute that is not hypostatized in a Gestalt is spatially higher than the mythic ground; it is hard to know whether its metaphorical transference to the dominant position first requires its being lowered to the primal democracy or whether it is already there. For this reason Borges uses language that is inexplicable when the story is taken only in its real-life sense, and places conjecture where it is not called for, emphasizing the certainty of other points whose veracity is not at issue. He tells us that "perhaps in the infamous Paseo de Julio she saw herself multiplied in mirrors, published by lights, and denuded by hungry eyes" (*A*, 62; *Lab.*, 134). Emma, we must infer, *may* have done those things that only a fully reified object can do: be multiplied in mirrors and revealed by light, and denuded of any appended attributes: singularized. But it is "more reasonable to conjecture that at the beginning she wandered, unnoticed, through the indifferent market place" (*A*, 62; *Lab.*, 134). It is more likely, that is, that in the beginning she was one of the unnoticed denizens of the mythic underworld, a jailbird in Babylon.

In any case, Borges esoterically assures the reader that it is certain Emma achieved union with the primeval: "It is sure that in the afternoon she went to the waterfront" (*A*, 62; *Lab.*, 134). Because of the special nature of Emma's being, the usual symbols of hypostatization do not surround her. The only outstanding image in the rest of the story is attached to Loewenthal: he has a blond beard that is stained with blood as he dies. His miserliness indicates his dogmatic, traitorous existence; he is said to be more adept at hoarding money (coin, being) than at earning it.

It is significant that in the paragraph telling of Emma's embarkation upon the miserable adventure with the sailor, Borges uses the word *atributo* twice, in a manner that causes his reader to wonder why that particular word is chosen:

To relate with some degree of reality the events of that afternoon would be difficult and perhaps contrary to law.[13] An attribute of the infernal is unreality, an attribute that appears to mitigate its terrors and that perhaps aggravates them (*A*, 61–62; *Lab.*, 134).

This seems to be a deliberate hint as to the ideal identity of Emma. The passage again points to the return to the mythic formlessness in that Emma's experience is called "unreal"—that is, existing in objective fact but only dimly in her subjective consciousness. Consistently, during the moments with the sailor, she gives herself up to vertigo, one of the basic symbols of the mythic condition. Emma goes with the sailor through a labyrinth of doors and hallways to the room where she is violated in a dizzy unreality; when she emerges, she is like her father, degraded by outward circumstances. Getting on a bus, Emma observes that the parks and trees have not been "contaminated" by what has been done to her; in other words, her Gestalt remains unaltered despite her metaphorical elevation to predominance. The sailor had given her money, which she threw away, and this seems to signify that her hypostatization is not genuine.

Emma fulfills the justice of rhetoric in the manner of her killing

[13] To tell these events "with reality" would be *improcedente*: contrary to law, unrighteous, against the rules. Again, Borges seems to be telling us that his story is faithful to some ideational procedure, some "mental process."

Loewenthal, and the words that she utters at the end of the story place her beyond the reach of retributive justice—beyond human law and beyond ideal inconsistency. Conceptual justice has been done and anything more is inconceivable.

Borges frequently uses the expression *hacer fuego* (literally, to "make fire") in shooting cases, in preference to *disparar, fusilar,* or some other word meaning "to shoot." Tamayo and Ruiz-Díaz have noted (*Enigma,* 53) that both "Death and the Compass" and "The Dead Man" end in phrases that contain this expression, but they do not inquire precisely into the value of it. Fire, as I have said, symbolizes that activity of the mind which dictates the destiny of hypostats. It burns dogmas, creates and fosters ideal reality, and is often but not always alluded to in cases of shooting; but where it is lacking, the idea of fulmination often replaces it. In "Emma Zunz" we have the only case I can remember in which a diehard mental figment has to be shot repeatedly. Struck by one bullet, then two, Loewenthal began to curse. "The evil words did not abate; Emma had to fire [*hacer fuego*] again" (*A,* 65; *Lab.,* 136). It seems appropriate that Emma should have to fire three times to accomplish what Ulpiano Suárez and several others achieved with a single fulminating blast, for Emma is only an adjectival appurtenance substituting for a full-fledged being.

"The Secret Miracle"

At the beginning of this story Borges tells of a centuries-long chess game between two families, carried on in a tower. The idea is parallel with that of a whole year of mental activity hypostatized as an instant of time in the mind of one man. The stakes in the chess game are said to be enormous, perhaps infinite, but nobody can name them. This, in turn, is parallel to the protagonist's (Hladík's) belief that by perfecting his play, *The Enemies,* he can "rescue (in a symbolic way) what was fundamental in his life" (*F,* 163–164; *Lab.,* 91; *Fic.,* 147), and this play is finished in the instantaneous mental year that is given to him in the split second between the sergeant's order to fire and the shock of the bullets. The comparison of the ideal world with a game of chess is made often by Borges, and every chess game implies that the players are themselves chessmen on some larger board, and so on to infinity.

The idealist mind hypostatizes everything upon the substratal mythic ground. But it cannot hypostatize itself—only symbols of itself. Such a self-conscious mind, turning to art for self-knowledge ("Art must show a man his own face"), can only produce a circular work in which the last line repeats the first and starts the action over again. Such is the play which Jaromir Hladík is trying to write. It is in verse, for verse "prevents the spectators from forgetting unreality, which is a precondition of art" (*F*, 162; *Lab.*, 91; *Fic.*, 146). It will be the symbolic justification of Hladík, but it will also justify God (*F*, 164; *Lab.*, 92; *Fic.*, 147), for Hladík and his drama are symbols of the divine mind.

The inability of the mind to see itself except in its symbols (hypostatizations) is suggested in various ways. It is most graphically symbolized in Hladík's dream of the chess game in the tower: he dreams that he is the firstborn heir of one of the competing families; that he is running across a rainy desert on the way to the chess match, which cannot be put off;[14] and that he cannot remember the chessmen or the rules of play. To be on a rainy desert, unable to remember the materials or the rules of imagination, is to be in the primal mythic condition, prior to time, not yet hypostatizing the perceptible universe and, like the magician of the circular ruins, giving no "premeditation" to the imaginative act— bringing no preconceptions to it. To be running toward the game is an action parallel with Hladík's later precipitous movement toward the climactic instant of his death, which is synonymous with the

---

[14] Here we have the word *postergar*, to postpone, but also "to ignore the primacy of." The sentence can be taken to mean that Hladík cannot postpone the chess game or that he cannot ignore the ultimacy of it. Since the game is an analogy for Hladík's mental process, the phrase "impostergable jugada" finally points to the *involuntary* "omnipotence" of the human mind.

whole mental year in which he manipulates his theatrical characters in a pattern that "justifies" him. The race toward the game in the tower, and the request for the all-important instantaneous year, are his efforts to "make himself firm somehow in the fugitive substance of time" (*F*, 161; *Lab.*, 90; *Fic.*, 145). And this self-anchoring in time, through which the chess player symbolizes on a board or on a playwright's stage what he himself is, is again parallel to finding in the vast Library of Clementinum the tiny letter that is God (*F*, 164; *Lab.*, 92; *Fic.*, 147).

It is hardly surprising that critics choose to comment on little in this story except the fanciful idea that time can be stopped in the outer world while it continues in a man's consciousness. The implication of worlds within worlds and minds within greater minds is finally somewhat stupefying, just as the limits of subjective knowledge cause a continual circularizing that becomes wearing on the idealist. As he waits in prison, Hladík, like Asterion, is tired of conjecture: "At times he longed with impatience for the final discharge, which would redeem him, for good or ill, from his vain task of imagining" (*F*, 161; *Lab.*, 90; *Fic.*, 145).

Hladík is both a thinker and a thought—a hypostatizing hypostat. Logically, he can be represented by the symbols of hypostatization or by those of universality; he is the chessboard on which he plays his figures and is himself a figure on a bigger field of play. Borges has to handle the symbols deftly. Let us see how he does it:

Hladík dreams of running across a rainy desert—or more exactly, across the *sands* of a rainy desert. Then he wakes up. That *afternoon* he is *arrested*. This is often the first step downward that a hypostat takes toward "death." We learn then that his *blood* is Jewish. When they sentence him to death, Hladík feels *terror*. (Remember the priests in Babylon who enjoyed "terror and hope.") We have seen that a frequent manner of death among hypostats is shooting, and that to fire is to obliterate or forget ideas. When Hladík, a mental reality, hears his sentence of death by shooting, it occurs to him that hanging or decapitation would not terrify him, but that being shot is intolerable. In Borges' very technical, humorous, and linguistic scheme, hanging is suspension, and the suspension of an idea does not deny it a possible resurrection. To decapitate is only to create the esthetic ambiguity by the removal of the crown. Shooting is annihilation.

It takes a full page of the story to recount the plot of Hladík's play. In it there are a few of the usual symbols: a reference to "a vehemence of setting sun" and "the occidental sun," a clock that marks the evening hour of seven, and a cryptic statement that evening has not fallen despite the hour. There is a concluding sentence that describes subjective thought as being circular and disconnected from objective reality: "The drama has not occurred: it is the circular delirium which Kubin lives and relives interminably" (*F*, 163; *Lab.*, 91; *Fic.*, 147).

After praying to be allowed to finish his play before dying, Hladík sleeps again. He dreams that he is in the Library of Clementinum looking for God, who is in one of the letters in one of the four hundred thousand volumes. A reader comes in and leaves an atlas, calling it worthless. Hladík picks it up casually and sees a map of India, clearly to be associated with the universal and Oriental. The sentence is ambiguous: "He saw a map of India, dizzy" (*F*, 164; *Lab.*, 91; *Fic.*, 147). Is Hladík dizzy, or the map? Hladík, for he is close to a revelation. Lying on the map, hypostatic in its tiny particularity, is the letter which is God. Hladík touches it and a "ubiquitous voice" informs him that his request for time has been granted.

One would expect Hladík to be stood before the wall in the evening, with a slanting sun overhead, since he is a doomed hypostat. On the contrary, he is marched out to die at 8:44 A.M., for the instant is approaching when he will hypostatize his self-symbol and be "justified." Myth must be his backdrop in this moment, so it is noted that he is "on his feet against the wall." They move him forward a bit so that the (mythic) wall will not be splattered with his (hypostatic) blood. To show that myth is present during the instantaneous year to follow, Borges has the sky cloud up, and a drop of rain starts rolling down Hladík's cheek in the moment of the order to fire. The drop hangs there, motionless, and time and the physical world stand still for one year. When Hladík fits the last epithet into his drama, the drop of water falls and the German lead finds its mark.

Generically, this story can be linked with a number of others; it is intrinsically nearest, I think, to "The Lottery in Babylon" with its instantaneous, simultaneous, and infinite lotteries, or to "The Circular Ruins" with its dream within a dream.

"The House of Asterion"

What are the thoughts of a circular intellect like that of Hladík? What are the thoughts of a mind which, in order to be outside the "universe," has only to open its eyes to the illusory and chaotic outer world? I have already spoken of "The House of Asterion" as being the soliloquy of an idealist. Here I want only to add a few comments.

The symbols of hypostatization in this story are sparse; and, logically, they appear in direct application to Asterion himself. Asterion, to be more specific than before, is not the mind, but that inner faculty or "soul" which has the "mind" (a mass of perceptions) as its habitation and tool. Asterion is the Company of Babylon.

They accuse him of pride, he tells us: the pride of feeling omnipotent in his world, perhaps, for it is his world alone. "The fact is that I am unique" (A, 68; Lab., 139). They accuse him of misanthropy. He has never been able to retain the difference between one letter and another: he is unable to distinguish "things" as substantially distinct. They accuse him of madness: the madness, perhaps, of Funes and of Carlos Argentino Daneri (A, 161; Per., 147), or even the opposite madness of the Zahir-stricken Borges or of zur Linde. Asterion's labyrinthine house, in which he insists he is not a prisoner, which he *has* ventured out of, and whose infinite doors are always open, is his own mind—the universe as he is able to have it. Everything in it is repeated; any place is any other place. But there are two things that "seem to be only once": above, the intricate sun; below, Asterion. Perhaps Asterion created the sun, he says, and the stars and the enormous house. He no longer remembers.

Every nine years nine men enter the house so that I can liberate them from all evil. I hear their footsteps or their voices in the depth of the galleries of stone and I run joyfully to look for them. The ceremony lasts only a few minutes. One after another they fall without my bloodying my hands. Where they fell they remain, and the bodies help to distinguish one gallery from the others (A, 69; Lab., 140).

These nine men who come into the labyrinth every nine years[15] must be understood as entrants from the world of objective reality; they are the only thing in Asterion's life that he does not have inside the labyrinth, the only indication that there is a reality outside to which he can be related. When these visitors "fall," one after the other, they help to distinguish galleries; that is, when these "facts" are assimilated, they make categories of knowledge and perception distinguishable—or rather, their bodies do, for as the Symbolists have it, language is a dead body, all that is left of experience.

I do not know who they are, but I know that one of them prophesied in the hour of his death that someday my redeemer would come. Since then the solitude does not pain me, for I know that my redeemer lives and in the end will rise above the dust (A, 69; Lab., 140).

Some category of knowledge, outer reality, or prophetic intuition has foretold that Asterion's redeemer will come. "If my ear should capture all the sounds of the world, I would perceive his steps." He is already in the world. Remembering that dust is a symbol of the substratal myth, we may surmise that the redeemer who raises

[15] The myth of the Minotaur uses the number seven; Borges has changed it to nine. Seven is a symbol of perfection and ultimacy, and in Greek and indo-Germanic thought the number nine has always competed with it. (See Cassirer, *Symbolic Forms*, II, 145–146.)

himself above the dust will be a hypostatization or a revelation with the power to simplify and integrate the universe, for it is hoped that he will take Asterion to "a place with fewer galleries and fewer doors" (*A*, 70; *Lab.*, 140). Knowledge is redemption, salvation; and salvation comes with death. As the false Villari turned his face to the wall, "the Minotaur scarcely defended himself" (*A*, 70; *Lab.*, 140). The death of Asterion is intellectual death. The redeemer is a world-replacing Zahir. Appropriately, Theseus returns from killing Asterion carrying a bloody sword.

The conventional symbols are few. The Minotaur himself is a *bull*, and he is killed with a bronze[16] *sword* from which Theseus wipes the *blood* in the *morning sun*.

"The Approach to Almotásim"

I feel I should remind the reader that although I may seem to offer my interpretations of an inner motif in Borges' stories as if they were explanations of whole inner structures, this is not the case. Borges is too complex, his style too exquisite, his structures too intricate, to be reduced to anything so simple. But I think it would be an error not to say that the motif I describe is almost ubiquitous, usually salient, at times comprising the structure and determining the movement of the story.

"The Approach to Almotásim" may be said to represent Borges' entry into the field of fantastic narrative. It was first published in 1936 as a part of his *History of Eternity*. This book, as César Fernández Moreno says (*Esquema de Borges*, p. 16), closes the essay stage of Borges' career. The account of the student's search for Almotásim (Al-Mu'tasim) makes up only about half the "story."

---

[16] As with the number nine, which occurs with some frequency, I have excluded bronze from the group of symbols discussed in this study. Bronze is alluded to fairly often; Funes had a face of bronze, for example. It is apparently a symbol of the fundamental, ancient, and universal. Other recurrent symbols which I have not discussed (which I cannot categorize with sufficient confidence) are the numbers eight and nineteen, the color green, and *losanges* (lozenges or rhombs).

Or to say it better, the account comprises the story, which is set in the middle of a pseudo-commentary on an imaginary Indian novel. The plot of the fictitious novel is the central element, and around it Borges groups little bundles of hints and decoys as to its meaning.

Again we must visualize, as Borges clearly does in this story, the pyramidal form of thought. But here it is a pyramid whose last stone or apical termination is missing. Borges begins the interior "novel" by posing two things in opposition: the One God of Islam (a completed pyramid) and the many gods of the Hindus. The student, who is never named, denies the One God (*F*, 36; *Fic.*, 38); he "disbelieves in the Islamic faith of his fathers." He becomes embroiled in a riot between Moslems and Hindus ("God the indivisible against the Gods"). He kills a Hindu, afterwards reflecting that he has murdered in the name of something whose existence he denies (*F*, 37–38; *Fic.*, 39). "He reflects that he has shown himself capable of killing an idolater, but not of knowing with certainty whether the Moslem is more right than the idolater."

The police who intervene to break up this battle are, appropriately, half asleep (*F*, 37; *Fic.*, 38): half dreaming, I infer, because they *intervene* between a hypostat (the One God) and a crowd of epithets or attributes without a semblance of order.

The student flees, crosses two railroads or the same one twice, climbs a wall, and enters a disorderly garden in the middle of which there is a circular tower. Before reaching the tower he is attacked by "una chusma de perros color de luna (a lean and evil mob of mooncoloured hounds),"[17] which is an apt way of making a symbolic reference to the multiplied Hindu gods, for dogs are hypostat symbols and the color yellow is associated in Borges' stories with everything Oriental, circular, universal. The student "seeks shelter in the tower," which foreshadows his success in finding Almotásim and his return, perhaps, to the Islamic One God.

[17] The English is Borges'. The fictitious novel is supposedly in English.

On the roof of the tower a filthy man is vigorously urinating by the light of the moon. He makes his living by stealing the gold teeth out of bodies left in the tower. He has all the qualities—he *is* all the qualities—that are antithetical to the one that later sends the student in search of Almotásim.

The student sleeps, then wakes "with the sun now high," and finds that the filthy man has robbed him of a number of things including some coins, "some rupees of silver." The thief had spoken earlier, in very vituperative language, of a certain woman in Palanpur. The student reasons that vilification by such a man is tantamount to praise, and he resolves to go in search of the woman. So the search for Almotásim really begins here as a reaction against that which is not Almotásim.

Here we can begin to suspect that what is later called Almotásim is but the ultimate or pure form of something that exists in the student himself, and the parable of the Simurg at the end of the story bears this out. The student falls among vile people and becomes one of them. But one day he perceives a mitigation in that infamy—"a tenderness, an exaltation, a silence in one of the abhorrent men" (*F*, 39; *Fic.*, 40). In other words, he sees in one of the depraved men a good quality which, in that man, is only a minor or subordinated attribute, as it is in the student himself. The student reasons:

At some point on the earth there is a man from whom this clarity proceeds; at some point on the earth there is a man who is equivalent to that clarity (*F*, 39; *Fic.*, 40).

This is to say that in some configuration of reality this quality is not a subordinate trait but a ruling god; this shared characteristic somewhere comprises a form that subsumes the individuals who share it. The more of it a man has, the closer he will be to the apex of the pyramid which culminates in that form:

In proportion to the closeness with which the interrogated men have known Almotásim, their divine portion is greater, but it is understood that they are only mirrors. The technicalities of mathematics are applicable: the loaded novel of Bahadur is an ascending progression whose final terminus is the foreshadowed "man who is called Almotásim" (*F*, 39; *Fic.*, 40).

The immediate precursor of Almotásim is a happy Persian bookseller, and just below him is a saint. After years, the student arrives at the pinnacle of the pyramidal search: a curtain-covered door, behind which is a resplendence. He knocks, the "incredible" voice of Almotásim bids him come in, he throws back the curtain and steps forward, and the "novel" ends.

What the student has found, in our mechanical terms, is the completed abstraction or hypostatization of a reality which the student has chosen to elevate to momentary supremacy. If the student had determined to search for Balidur the Bad, let us say, instead of Almotásim the Good, he would have searched through the same men, building a pyramid out of the same stones, but with each stone turned in such a way that a different feature would be emphasized. Each stone *is* its emphasized feature. All men, in the moment of being good, are Almotásim; his name is Goodness.

The student himself is Almotásim, in one sense (*F*, 43; *Fic.*, 43), and Almotásim is God in another sense (*F*, 40; *Fic.*, 41), and he is a god who accommodates himself to every believer, being everything to everyone (*F*, 40; *Fic.*, 41). The parable of the Simurg gives the overall form that subsumes these sundry speculations.[18] The tale goes thus: The birds go off in search of their king, whose name means "thirty birds." When they reach the place where he is, all have died except thirty. "They are the Simurg . . . and the Simurg is each one of them and all." Borges adds: "Everything in the intelligible heavens is everywhere. Any thing is every thing" (*F*, 43; *Fic.*, 43). Whether everything is one thing or another depends on the angle of vision only, the momentary emphasis, the provisional Zahir. Some part of every man is his subjective god; some

[18] The parable of the Simurg is given in a footnote (*F*, 42; *Fic.*, 43), is mentioned (*OI*, 111; *Oth. Inq.*, 77), and is told at length (*M*, 134–135).

part of the subjective gods is God. A concept, according to epistemologists, is what all conceptions of a thing have in common.

"Story of the Warrior and the Captive"

This is not one of Borges' fantastic stories. The histories of
the German warrior Droctulft, who left barbarism for the city, and
of the captive English girl who renounced civilization for barbarism, are for Borges the same history. Both of these people
heeded "an impulse deeper than reason . . . which they would not
have known how to justify" (*A*, 52; *Lab.*, 131). This impetus and a
number of symbols seem to be the only elements which link this
story with the motif that concerns us here. It is the only thing
Droctulft and the girl have in common. At the end of the narrative
Borges states that the two faces of this *coin* (*A*, 52; *Lab.*, 131) are
the same in God's eyes. Perhaps we could say that the impetus he
speaks of is that same undefinable, destiny-dealing Company of
Babylon.

Droctulft is a Lombard soldier; he came from the swamps and
forests beyond the Danube and the Elbe and is "loyal to his captain
and his tribe, not to the universe." He worships an idol, Hertha,
that is carried around in a cart. But when the wars take him to
Ravenna,

He sees a conjunct that is multiple without disorder; he sees a city, an
organism made of statues, of temples, of habitations, of stairways, of
urns, of spires, of regular and open spaces (*A*, 48; *Lab.*, 128).

It is not the city's beauty that impresses him; it is like a complex
machine whose purpose is unknown to him, but in whose design he
senses an immortal intelligence. He knows that this city "is worth
more than his gods, more than his sworn faith, and more than all
the swamps of Germany" (*A*, 49; *Lab.*, 128).

Droctulft abandoned—in fact, turned against—his own people.
But this does not make him a traitor: "He was not a traitor . . . he
was an enlightened one, a convert." He knows that in this city he

will be a dog, a child, and that he will never begin to understand it. He is like Tzinacán in that he is willing to be reduced to nothing for the sake of this revelation; he is like zur Linde in his willingness to be sacrificed if only this wonder can be glorified in the act; he is like Nils Runeberg, who wants only to be immolated before his God. What Droctulft sees is at once an Alephic *multum in parvo* and somehow also a Zahir—that which is not the universe but is altogether as if it were.

The captive girl also comes out of the primeval chaos—the desert —to a frontier settlement. Offered a chance to escape back to civilization, she prefers the life of the Indian on the pampa. Borges' grandmother, who tried to persuade her to return to her own people, sees her one day at a *rancho* where a man is cutting the throat of a sheep. The girl is riding by on horseback "as if in a dream," and she jumps from the horse to drink the warm blood, either as a sign and a challenge or because she can no longer restrain herself from doing such things. The English girl has left her own kind, to be an egregious rebel against the orderly world that Droctulft loved, but she is no more a traitor than he.

For Borges, betrayal is something that happens in the mind, not in the outer world. No one is a traitor unless he represents an *ideal* reality. Both the warrior and the captive are faithful to something on the ideal plane. Droctulft has abandoned mental chaos (the flat marshes of Germany) for something that is structured and fixed, a kind of total Zahir that puts order into the universe, although it does not make it comprehensible; he wants to be subordinate to something eternal, a part of invariable reality. The girl, however, rejects a structured eternity in favor of an egregious, provisional existence. She drinks the symbol of ideal, insecure being and of mortality: blood. The butchered sheep reminds us of the sacred bulls slaughtered by the narrator of "Babylon." The girl, on horseback and in "a dream," is free in a way that Droctulft cannot be. Droctulft was converted to a classical world-view; the

English girl turned her back on that and remained a Romantic.[19]

"Biography of Tadeo Isidoro Cruz (1829–1874)"

Another traitor who is not a traitor is Tadeo Isidoro Cruz, whose story is also to be excluded from the fantastic category. It is a story about a mind, not about its contents. But its central elements are as if taken from that same store which produced Borges' most mystifying allegories. Some of the lines that critics are fondest of quoting are these:

(There awaited him, secret in the future, a lucid, fundamental night: the night in which he finally saw his own face, the night in which he finally heard his name. Well understood, that night sums up his history; to say it better, an instant in that night, because actions are our symbol). Any destiny, no matter how long and complex it may be, consists in reality of a single moment: the moment in which a man knows forever who he is (A, 55; Per., 163).

One night that contains, in effect, all nights; one instant that sums up all the instants of a man's life; one act that is a man's total symbol—all have the form of a Zahir that is also an Aleph: a point selected out of an infinity, representing that infinity so ultimately that in effect all the details of it are present.

Cruz was a gaucho. He had his brushes with the law. Then he became a part of that law and, with others, pursued the outlaw Martín Fierro. In the middle of a fight Cruz suddenly realized "that one destiny is no better than another, but that every man ought to heed the one he carries within" (A, 56–57; Per., 164). The Company is again casting the lots. When he realized that he and

[19] In "The Shape of the Sword" Borges seems to justify my use of "Romantic," perhaps as a synonym for "idealist." The narrator, speaking of his beloved Ireland, says "we were, I suspect, Romantics. Ireland was for us not only the Utopian future and the intolerable present, but a bitter and dear mythology; it was the circular towers and red marshes." (F, 131; Lab., 68; Fic., 118). These latter images are oxymora signifying idealist hypostatization —conscious fictionmaking.

Martín Fierro were in effect the same man, "it dawned on the law-less plain" and he changed sides. All changes in the structure of reality are likely to take place at dawn, less often at evening twi-light; and when it dawns on a plain, a swamp, the sea, the horizon, or anything else that is flat or vast, the time is propitious for hypostats to rise and fall, or for unjustified dualities to merge. It would have been a consistent and appropriate image if Borges had chosen to insert at the end of this story some reference to the breaking of an evil mirror or the destruction of an impious echo.

"Averroes' Search"

"The story of a defeat" is what Borges calls this narrative about Averroes' inability to arrive at a proper conception of "tragedy" and "comedy." Analogous to this defeat is the "red Adam that cannot stand up" in "The Circular Ruins." Mental impotence is betokened in various ways throughout the story and is made in some degree analogous with the dichotomy between language and reality. For example:

The Koran . . . is one of the attributes of God, like His piety; it is copied in a book, it is pronounced with a tongue, it is remembered in the heart, and the language and the signs and the scripture are the work of men, but the Koran is irrevocable and eternal (A, 95; Lab., 151).

And: ". . . the moon of Bengal is not the same as the moon of Yemen, but it can be described with the same words" (A, 96; Lab., 151). Borges gives us, in this way, a suggestion of Platonic form variously incarnated in language and matter. To the words about the Koran, above, he adds: "Averroes . . . could have said that the mother of the Book is something like its Platonic model" (A, 95; Lab., 151). The conception of tragedy and comedy to which Averroes finally attains is of the same mold, being only one articu-lation of the form, and failing, therefore, to correspond to it ab-solutely. Borges says in this regard:

The image that a single man can form is one which does not correspond to a single man. There is an infinite number of things in the world; any one of them can be equated with any other (*A*, 99; *Lab.*, 153–154).

But this does not totally negate the usefulness of Averroes' idea of the meaning of "comedy" and "tragedy," for a form is equatable, as a matter of practicality, with any of its manifestations. Speaking of verses, Averroes comments: "I know of some which, like music, are all things for all men" (*A*, 99; *Lab.*, 154). Borges is highly conscious of the variable articulation of ideal reality and is forever alluding to the apostle Paul, who was all things to all men (1 Corinthians 9:22).

The symbols of hypostatization that occur in this story are of the usual kind, but at the same time are highly original. Borges makes a passing allusion to the nature of momentary god-making that prefigures the end of the story, where Averroes disappears because Borges has stopped thinking about him. As Averroes puzzles over the meaning of the obscure words, his attention is caught by a sound: "From that studious distraction a sort of melody distracted him." Very clever, this—the introduction of an example of form (music) immediately before presenting the form of the hypostat. The "sort of melody" is a boy imitating the high-pitched prayer call of a muezzin. One boy stood on another's shoulders pretending to be a muezzin atop a minaret. Another boy, "abject in the dust, and kneeling," played the role of congregation. This upright projection above the dust is momentary; it soon dissolves and there is competition to see which of the boys gets to be the muezzin next: "They all wanted to be the muezzin; nobody wanted to be the congregation or the tower" (*A*, 93; *Lab.*, 149).

From this scene Borges takes us with Averroes to a soirée in the house of Farach, which begins with the coming of the evening twilight. In the garden the guests talk of roses. One guest says that in the gardens of Hindustan there is a *red rose* whose petals bear letters which spell out the Moslem creed: "There is no other god like the one God. Mohammed is the Apostle of God." It is called the perpetual rose. The redoubled image "red rose" is appropriate; this flower perpetually bears the supreme Zahir, or dogma, of the Moslems.

The boys playing muezzin and the discussion of roses do not have any overt connection, of course, with Averroes' search—nor, in fact, does most of the rest of the narrative about the soirée, except that one guest, Abulcásim, relates having seen a stage performance during his many travels; that story told in action remains a mystery to him. As an Arab he cannot grasp its purpose or value.

After the discussion Averroes returns home, where a red-haired slave girl has been tortured by others with black hair; but Averroes "will not know it until afternoon." The symbol is parallel to Averroes' defeat; he has failed to grasp "tragedy" and "comedy," but he thinks he has understood them and records: " 'Aristu (Aristotle) applies the name of tragedy to panegyrics and the term comedy to satires and anathemas' " (A, 100; Lab., 155). If Averroes had fully understood the two types of drama, the red-haired girl presumably would have prevailed over the others, or at least would have fended them off.

Borges then speaks of his own defeat in being unable to imagine Averroes adequately, and again offers a symbol of the Zahir: "I felt what must have been felt by that god mentioned by Burton, who set out to create a bull and a created a buffalo" (A, 101; Lab., 155).

"The Library of Babel"

The infinite Library of Babel is a strikingly effective symbol of the inconceivable universe and a good example of an Aleph-Zahir—a conceptual substitute for the universe which preserves the details. The elements that enter into the description of the Library are all quite concrete and conceivable, but the description delivers to us the *import* (the inconceivability) of the universe, not the conceivability of the thing described.

The Idealism of Berkeley and his followers is visible throughout the story; but Schopenhauer is most palpably present: The world is my idea, subject to my will. Schopenhauer and Vaihinger could have written the story.

"The Library of Babel" contains relatively little in the way of motif-imagery, because the world view that dictates the story is itself dictated by that motif; that is, the story is a testimonial not to the form but to the necessity of hypostatization. I will speak only of those few symbols that make this point.

Borges shows us that the Library contains not only the *things* of the universe, but its history and its future as well. Time is included. Countless men have worn out their lives and their eyesight trying to decipher and organize the books; many have killed themselves; various sects have started movements; there are philosophies and ideas and interpretations; but all comes to nothing.

An unmitigated depression ensues, based on the suspicion that the only books of any value, which can give the key to all the books, are inaccessible; truth cannot be known. So one group of men proposed giving the initiative to the words in the books—or more precisely, they proposed to manipulate the letters endlessly and give chance the opportunity to turn up something meaningful:

A blasphemous sect suggested that the searching be stopped and that all men shuffle letters and symbols until they formed, with the help of an improbable gift of chance, those canonical books (*F*, 91; *Lab.*, 55; *Fic.*, 84).

The authorities forbade this, and the sect disappeared. But the surrender to chance was not thwarted; it is here that Borges shows what he believes to be the normal, natural, and finally inescapable human necessity—that of creating one's own universal order:

The sect disappeared, but in my childhood I saw old men who for long periods hid themselves in the latrines, with some metal disks in a prohibited dicebox, and weakly imitated the divine disorder (*F*, 91; *Lab.*, 55; *Fic.*, 84).

The Red Hexagon is the location of certain books that are

"omnipotent, learned, and magic" (*F*, 92; *Lab.*, 56; *Fic.*, 85). The omnipotent books are "of smaller format than the natural ones"—minor or simplified books that magically contain more than is in them.

The total book, which is "the perfect compendium of all the others," is the object of universal search. We must think of it as an Aleph, not a Zahir, because it is perfect; it contains the entire universe in detail. Borges prays that someone, sometime, has read that book:

... I implore the unknown gods that a man—only one, though it were thousands of years ago!—may have examined and read it. If honor and wisdom and happiness are not to be mine, let them be for others. Let heaven exist, though my place be in hell. Let me be outraged and annihilated, but let your enormous Library be justified in one instant, in one being (*A*, 93; *Lab.*, 57; *Fic.*, 86).

Borges' abnegation before the great Library is remindful of this same attitude in Droctulft, who worshipped a city; in Tzinacán, whom the universe left without an identity or will of his own; and in Otto zur Linde, whose story follows.

"Deutsches Requiem"

The narrator of "Deutsches Requiem" is the Nazi commandant of a concentration camp, Otto Dietrich zur Linde (*die Linde*, lime tree), who has hypostatized one value and subordinated the rest of the universe, including himself and his country. Apparently the thing he has raised to supremacy is war; and war, I believe, is one of Borges' symbols for the chaos and flux of the idealist mentality. Paradoxical as it may seem, zur Linde's fanatical, unbending attitude may be representative of the idealist's dogged enmity against esthetic and intellectual intransigence; for idealism, which denies fixations, is itself a fixation by virtue of its being a point of view. Borges would not hesitate to acknowledge this.

The personality of zur Linde is Prussian; it suggests everything hard and rigid: iron, the sword, the will. He is brought into a trinity through which Borges symbolizes three configurations of mind: alongside Zur Linde are Walt Whitman and the fictitious poet David Jerusalem. In discussing these men's views of the universe Borges gives his reader the clue that the story is about ways of conceiving reality, not about Nazis and Jews and a Germany gone wrong. Whitman, the narrator opines, was a poet whose vision of the universe was somewhat transcendental and detached, while that of David Jerusalem, who he admits is his own superior, is a vision of the world from within the world:

Whitman celebrates the universe in a manner that is preliminary, general, almost indifferent; Jerusalem rejoices in each thing, with meticulous love. He never perpetrates enumerations or catalogues. I can still repeat many hexameters of that profound poem entitled *Tse Yang, Painter of Tigers*, which is, so to speak, striped with tigers, loaded and crisscrossed with transversal, silent tigers (*A*, 85; *Lab.*, 144).

In these words Borges attributes to Whitman the characteristics of the nominalist or Alephic world view; Whitman enumerates and catalogues, like Dante and like Carlos Argentino Daneri. David Jerusalem, however, is Platonic and Zahiristic, though in a sense his approach to reality is like that of the idealist, being a continual movement from one thing to another. But his essential characteristic is given by Borges: ". . . he had dedicated his genius to the praise of happiness" (*A*, 85; *Lab.*, 144). Happiness, I suggest again, is a Zahir-symbol—or rather, a symbol of ideation, as it is in "The Babylonian Lottery." David Jerusalem represents a mentality that is able to turn its attention, with momentarily total dedication, upon every idea or perception, to the exclusion of the rest of the universe. Borges equates this momentary hypostatization with love, with tenderness, with pity; and this should remind us of the quest for the ultimate, revelatory Zahir, Almotásim, whose existence was first suggested by the occurrence of a tenderness in a man. Let us remember, too, that Jerusalem, the maker of Zahirs-in-panorama, is like the Borges who stood before the random photographs of

Beatriz with adoration for each. The story hints that David Jerusalem is perhaps a symbol of something in zur Linde himself that has to be killed if he is to become a totally dedicated disciple of Mars:

I do not know whether Jerusalem understood that if I destroyed him, it was to destroy my own compassion. In my eyes he was not a man, not even a Jew; he had been transformed into a detested area of my soul (A, 86–87; Lab., 145).

Borges the idealist must destroy in himself the tendency to settle his "love" upon any particular view of reality, any special interpretation of the world, any single esthetic. He contains the longing for intellectual security, for the certainty of dogma, just as zur Linde contained Jerusalem. So how does the idealist destroy the Zahir-making inclination? By giving it enough rope to hang itself; by allowing the Zahir to become ridiculous and insane in its singularity and rigidity:

. . . there is nothing in the world that is not the germ of a possible Hell; a face, a word, a compass, a cigarette advertisement could drive a person mad if he was not able to forget it. Wouldn't a man be insane who continuously imagined a map of Hungary? I made up my mind to apply this principle. . . . At the end of 1942 Jerusalem lost his reason; on the first of March, 1943, he managed to kill himself (A, 86; Lab., 145).

A footnote tells us that it was also on the first day of March, 1939, that zur Linde's leg was pierced by two bullets, and that later it was amputated; an apparent parallel with the amputation of Jerusalem from the Nazi's soul, accomplished in the usual manner that Borges applies to the death of a Zahir: shooting, or piercing.

Borges gives many indications that he himself is zur Linde. Like Borges, the German can name illustrious ancestors who died in battle, made studies, and wrote books; one of his ancestors was a Hebraist, and Borges has a Jewish forebear. In his youth zur Linde had two passions: music and metaphysics. He had delved into poetry. He loves Schopenhauer, who led him away from religion, and he likes Shakespeare and Brahms for "the infinite variety of their worlds" (*A*, 82; *Lab.*, 143). This nominalism that he finds in them conduces, paradoxically, to monism; that is, the proliferation of things-in-themselves drives the intellect toward seeking a final order, or single substance, that accounts for all. In any case, zur Linde finds it difficult to appreciate things-in-themselves, which is a Platonic fault: "Individually, my comrades were detestable to me; in vain I tried to reason that under the high purpose that called us together, we were not individuals" (*A*, 83; *Lab.*, 143).

With the death of Jerusalem, zur Linde's self-molding is complete; he is unredeemably dedicated to his Zahir, which is—in the present interpretation—an idealist rejection of Zahirism. The Nazi immolates himself before his god. That god, that final value which is destroying Germany and zur Linde himself, is symbolically called violence or war and is opposed to what zur Linde calls Judeo-Christian timidity. This is consistent with logic. Zahirism in the sense of the making of destructive myths destroyed the Third Reich, and in Borges' view, rigid Judeo-Christian monotheism is pure Zahirism. Germanic mythmaking before World War I was denounced by Vaihinger (*'As If,'* p. *xxxix*), who called it a destructive "optimism" and predicted that it would cause Germany's downfall. When Borges says, therefore, that zur Linde's god—idealism, symbolized as War or Violence—was destroying Germany, we should understand that Germany was destroyed by the Zahiristic, "optimistic," Utopian motivation of the Nazis. Again the old saying: the Germans are forever making myths and the French are forever denying them.

Zur Linde speculates about why he is strangely happy at Germany's approaching defeat. It is not because he feels secretly guilty, not because he is tired of the struggle, and not because resentment would be "blasphemous against the universe," but because his god—the subjective universe, the idealist Will—is justified. He explains this by appealing to the dictum that all men are Platonists or Aristotelians—two forms, let us say, that are transcended in idealism—and by inferring from this that all men are the tools of Destiny. The destruction of "Judaism" and "Christianity" —that is, of any monolithic and moralistic world view—is the supreme good for which zur Linde will gladly sacrifice himself and his country. In the same words with which he appealed for the justification of the great Library of Babel, he prays for the prevalence of the Company, the will, the power to create and destroy (mentally), here symbolized as violence:

The important thing is that violence should reign, not the servile Christian timidities. If victory and injustice and happiness are not for Germany, let them be for other nations. Let heaven exist though our place be in hell (*A*, 89; *Lab*., 147).

Otto zur Linde, like his Germanic forebear Droctulft, is a man who is no longer loyal to his captain and his tribe, but to the universe.

"Three Versions of Judas"

Judas, far from being a vile traitor, sacrificed his soul for the glory of God:

The ascetic, for the greater glory of God, vilifies and mortifies the flesh; Judas did the same thing to the spirit. He renounced honor, good, peace, the kingdom of heaven, just as others, less heroically, renounce pleasure. . . . He acted with gigantic humility, believing himself unworthy to be good. . . . Judas sought Hell because the blessedness of the Lord was enough for him (*F*, 172; *Lab*., 97; *Fic*., 154).

This self-humiliating Judas looks on the surface like another Droctulft, zur Linde, or Tzinacán. The man who puts forth the theory that Judas betrayed Christ not for greed but for God's glory is Nils Runeberg, who is himself a kind of nothing, a *nil*, remembered now only by heresiologists. He died of a ruptured aneurism, like Herbert Ashe, who also is barely remembered.

The terrible idea that Judas destroyed his own soul out of love for God, and that God permitted and even ordained it, would not appeal to Borges if it did not have the form of elevation-subordination, the existence of a reality at the expense of other realities, the preeminence of the wilfully erected and arbitrarily supported truth. The heretical theologian Runeberg reasons thus: God reduced himself for man's glorification. He had to do it perfectly, completely; he had to *be* Judas, commit the only crime that has nothing good in it, and suffer the worst possible fate, the loss of his (God's!) own soul. This reasoning is based in part on the exercise of a device very typical of Borges: the movement of reality from one plane of being to another. The reduction of God to the condition of man can only be paralleled by the reduction of man to the condition of a demon in hell. In form, therefore, Judas in some way reflects Jesus. Nils Runeberg believes that by discovering the horrible name of God he has possibly committed the unpardonable sin. He is happy, and hopes for the grace to share hell with the Redeemer. In showing how a sophism can be carried to an unthinkable and fascinating extreme, Borges again testifies to the paradoxical impotence and omnipotence of the human mind.

I suggest only a few parallels by way of interpretation. Here Runeberg's God is his Redeemer, as Theseus is the redeemer of Asterion. Runeberg's discovery of God's name—his discovery of the Hundredth Name, let us say, which has power to fulminate the universe—is the discovery of the ultimate Zahir; it is called "possibly the unpardonable sin," which may mean the irretrievable last step to intellectual death. And this death, we remember, is also salvation. To be with the redeemer—to have the comfort of an unshakable Zahir—is both a hell and a heaven, as Borges so repeatedly tells us in symbol.

"Abenjacán the Bojarí, Dead in his Labyrinth"

A red labyrinth is a rare oxymoron. A red man in a yellow labyrinth would be more likely; but here we have a red house constructed by a man with lemon-colored skin and a saffron beard.

"Abenjacán the Bojarí" (*A*, 123–134) is a kind of police story like "Death and the Compass" and the two have a few features in common. If we can believe the version told by Unwin in the story, a man has trapped and killed another man and made off with his money; if we believe the version accepted by the townspeople, a ghost hunted a man down, took revenge on him, and stole his treasure.

Unwin's version is much more likely, and Borges apparently wants us to accept it. It is a clever reversal of the events told in the brief story that follows "Abenjacán" in the collection *El Aleph*—the short parable "The Two Kings and the Two Labyrinths." This parable, according to a footnote, is the sermon preached by Rector Allaby in the story of the Bojarí. In this sermon-parable the King of Babylon puts his guest, the King of the Arabs, into a man-made labyrinth and he finds his way out only with divine help. Later, the Arab gets revenge by losing the Babylonian in God's labyrinth, the desert. In "Abenjacán" a betrayal in the desert is requited with a murder in a man-made labyrinth.

But if we had no other indication as to which of the two versions of Abenjacán's death is the true one, Borges' symbolic hints would guide us. They point to the accuracy of Unwin's account.

In the version told by Dunraven and generally believed in spite of its incredibility, the desert chieftain Abenjacán flees across the desert with an ill-gotten treasure, accompanied by his cowardly vizir Zaid. To avoid sharing the treasure, he stabs Zaid in his sleep, and the dying man swears to track him down. Abenjacán builds, in England, a labyrinthine red house on top of a hill by the sea, telling the local vicar that it is to protect him from the ghost of Zaid. One day Abenjacán bursts into the vicar's house to tell him that Zaid has come into the labyrinth and killed his servant and a guardian lion. Later, the vicar finds Abenjacán dead and his treasure stolen. Abenjacán had said that he obliterated Zaid's face with a rock when he killed him in the desert; now Abenjacán, the servant, and the lion are found mutilated in the same way.

But Unwin, hearing this story, discredits it. According to him, it could only have happened this way: Zaid the coward would not have been sleeping during the pursuit in the desert; it was he who betrayed Abenjacán, but not by killing him. He abandoned him, stole half his treasure, buried the rest, and built the conspicuous labyrinth in order to attract Abenjacán and kill him with less personal risk. He obliterated the face so it would appear to be he, Zaid (posing in England as the other), who was dead. Zaid took the treasure, if any was left after building the house, and went off to recover the buried remainder. When he burst into the vicar's house, he had already killed the real Abenjacán.

This story is another that hardly belongs in the fantastic category. It is a fanciful mystery, but does not carry that strange aura that tells us Borges is really talking about something else. Nevertheless, the antagonists can be lifted to the ideal plane, where the symbols of reality corroborate Unwin's interpretation.

We saw in "The Cult of the Phoenix" that those who do not participate in the secret rite are scorned, and in "The Lottery in Babylon" we learned that those who do not take part in the lottery are treated as if they were cowardly. Zaid the cowardly vizir could not kill Abenjacán in the desert for lack of courage. Also, he could not or did not sleep ("To sleep is to be distracted from the world," A, 132). Abenjacán's name begins with A, and Zaid's with Z. Since a labyrinth is symbolic of the universe, and since redness symbolizes life, or predominance, a red labyrinth may be taken as the symbol of a Gestalt that is altogether "alive"—not yet organized and dominated by a hypostat. An Aleph-like situation, a myth. Indeed, at the beginning of the story—long after the murder, when the house is vacant and deteriorating—the building is described as a *caballeriza venida a menos*: a crumbling stable, or, in our necessarily technical terms, a stable that has *come to less*. "Caballeriza" carries the connotation of "a collection of horses." Horses are hypostat symbols; a stable or group of them suggests an Aleph or something like it. This Alephic reality is predominant (red) until the timid Zaid (Zahir) kills it—kills Abenjacán—and this is shown in the fact that at the end of the story the red house has faded to a rose color; again, it has "come to less." While it was red, Zaid's beard was yellow, like his skin, but with enough red to make it a bit orange. We are not told, but it is probable that after he killed Abenjacán and left not a single *coin* in the house, his beard became redder. The ship on which Abenjacán had come (the *Rose of Sharon*) sailed away for the *Red* Sea with Zaid aboard, and Borges finally attributes to him the color of the labyrinth he built: he is called "the vermilion man" (*A*, 133). As a Zahir substitutes for the universe, Borges tells us that Zaid has become Abenjacán: "He pretended to be Abenjacán, he killed Abenjacán, and finally he *was Abenjacán*" (*A*, 134). As we have seen in other stories, a Zahir has the pernicious power to simulate, kill, and replace the universe.

"The Man on the Threshold"

This is undoubtedly one of Borges' most enigmatic stories. There is little in it to indicate an intention on Borges' part to speak ambiguously of the ideal and real worlds, but he is faithful to the correspondence between men and ideas; he shows, as elsewhere, that the essential tension between a thing and its attributes is like the tension between a ruler and his people or between the winners and losers in the lottery. He carries the parallel even further and depicts the animosity, so to speak, between the willful and dynamic European and the abysmal, unchanging, "universal," and essentially passive Easterner. Some of the usual symbols appear: a reddish lute, yellow flowers, mentions of blood and violence, light (*claridad*), the sun, trees, nakedness, and others. With veiled significance, exactly the same words are used to describe an old beggar that are used to characterize another in the story called "The South." The story itself is suggestive of others in that it somehow dissolves time and repeats a history: an execution that occurred years before is recounted by the old beggar, and at the end of his account the narrator finds the body of the missing Glencairn, who has been executed.

To interpret the story would be to paraphrase an ingenious sophistry that I am not sure I comprehend. Let me only point out that the events of the narrative are consistent with the conceptual manipulation of the images and symbols we have been dealing with in other stories.

At least two metaphysical schemes present themselves; the first is perhaps too simple to satisfy: A hypostat that is inimical to its own attributes cannot last. The iron-fisted Glencairn, who was brought in by the government to quell the strife among Moslems, Sikhs, and Hindus in an Indian city, is too rigid and domineering to be tolerated. His tyranny is requited with a death sentence handed down by an insane judge; intelligible order is brought under judgment by chaos and destroyed.

The second is more palatable, but tenuous. First let me lay out the facts in the story. The narrator is looking for David Alexander Glencairn, the big Scotsman imported by the government to put down the religious riots. Glencairn was of an illustrious *warrior* clan, and in his *blood* he carried a tradition of *violence*. Like his namesakes, David and Alexander, he ruled with a scepter of *iron*. He had black hair. The *sun* has set when the narrator arrives at a public house looking for Glencairn. A celebration is going on. The narrator sees a *blind* man carrying a lute of *reddish* wood. Then he talks to an old man whom the years have polished as the waters wear away a stone. For this old man the present moment is hardly more than an indefinite sound; he lives in a larger time sphere. The old man tells the story of a man, apparently a duplicate of Glencairn, who was executed by the people years before. In that story the man imported to impose British law was tried in kangaroo court and the verdict was entrusted to an insane beggar. Insanity is somehow symbolic of the enigmatic East, where it is often revered as the blessing of God. It is also symbolic of obsession—the

Zahir. The insane beggar was one who walked the streets naked and "mocked the trees" (A, 148). His verdict was "guilty," and he killed the defendant—or someone did—with a knife in the throat. As the beggar's story is finished, the narrator comes upon an old man with a dirty sword; he has just killed Glencairn and is receiving homage from the people. He wears a garland of yellow roses.

I fasten on an abstract interpretation of the interrelationships of symbols that is consistent, at least, with Borges' system. Glencairn was brought into the city to put down the trouble between Sikhs and Moslems. Succeeding after a time, he became tyrannical; Sikhs and Moslems worked together for his downfall, and he disappeared. I have pointed out before that conflicting ideas require transcending fictions, while the absence of contradiction renders this transcendence impossible. With the coming of peace between the disputing sects, it is natural that Glencairn, who in a sense transcends them, should vanish. "The city and the district were at peace: Sikhs and Moslems had put aside the old discords and suddenly Glencairn disappeared" (A, 144). His ideal being, caused by conflict, is perhaps indicated in the tradition of "violence" that he carried in his "blood" (A, 144). In his being, that is, he carried the inevitability of his "alternation" or demise.

But what does Glencairn represent? Something more, surely, than a mere Zahir. I suggest that he stands for the thing that Otto zur Linde was totally dedicated to—a kind of intellectual variability, "war," estheticism, or idealism, that transcends rigid and contradictory points of view. The Indians in this story, while they represent the universal, traditional cultures of the world as opposed to the Zahir-prone Germanic or European dynamism, nevertheless appear here to be as unchanging as we conceive them to be. There is at least one oxymoronic image that seems to hint at this: the yellow roses that adorned the head of the executioner. Yellow, I have said before, is symbolic of the Alephic or universal; roses are a symbol of the Zahir. Glencairn's black hair, on the other hand, would be inexplicable in terms of Borges' system if it were not intended to mitigate his rigid aspect. Borges takes the trouble to point out, in the alternative story of the English governor killed years before, that the warring sects were of all kinds: monotheistic Sikhs, polytheistic Hindus, black Jews, monks, Koran experts, and doctors of law. Their irreconcilable points of view were transcended by their enmity toward Glencairn. Philosophical idealism would be out of place, noncompetitive, in a place like India. The strange combination of ideas expressed in one sentence seems to sum up the story somehow: "Sikhs and Moslems put aside the old discords and suddenly Glencairn disappeared."

"The Shape of the Sword" and "Theme of the Traitor and the Hero"

If we take too much of Borges' fiction at one sitting we grow tired of trying to decide who is who, who really killed whom, and whether a man died at one moment or at another time years later—and whether he is a hero or a coward, a convert or a traitor. Only by lifting the action to the ideal plane and speaking of the consciousness as a stage on which the drama is acted out by images and conceptions that obey the rules of thought, not the physical and social laws we live by, can we put consistency into Borges' tales and justify the opinion that they are fantastic without being untrue. Doing this removes Borges' fictions from any relation with morality or immorality and from any connection with conventional values, leaving only one criterion of good and evil: freedom or, in a sense, courage. The only law of the universe is the law of the Company's omnipotence, and every man is his own Company. The Company must be free, and must have the courage, to raise to momentary "glory" those facets of reality which it needs for its own preservation and integrity.

"The Shape of the Sword" is another realistic story that carries little of the implied other plane; nevertheless the other plane is present. John Vincent Moon's crime is that he has betrayed the friend who helped him. In the ideal realm he has betrayed him in a different sense of the word: he has "revealed" him, displaced him, become him. The Irishman who tells Borges the story of the traitor confesses at the end that he is himself the miserable John Vincent Moon. Because he has acted this way, he can never again be trustworthy in the moral sense, and in the ideal sense he can never be an unequivocal quality capable of hypostatization; he is as useless to the ideal Company as he is to the Irish cause. He is doomed forever to duality, half-existence, inner division—to the status of an attribute that can never give its name to a Gestalt.

For this reason he has a gray mustache, not even a beard; his very name, Moon, indicates the half-light in which he lives; and the half-moon carved on his face is the symbol of his moral coward-ice and his ideal or cosmic impotence. On his plantation in Brazil he worked alongside his own inferiors, his peons. Like the stranger who called himself Villari in "The Wait," he received no letters. Ordinarily we find the color red ascribed to men (hypostats) against a background of landscapes and structures that are yellow, gray, etc. But in this story, in "Abenjacán," in "Theme of the Traitor and the Hero," and in "The South" we find red things that fade and yellow or grayish *men*, some of whom become a bit red-dish. The Irishman is from La Colorada (*colorado* means "red-dish"). His narrative, told to Borges, has the Irish revolution as its setting, as does "Theme of the Traitor and the Hero," and in both these stories there are oxymoronic red swamps serving as back-drops to circular towers and gray hills. In both stories there are references to the transmigration of souls, once a Celtic belief. Borges seems to attribute to Ireland the quality and the aura of fic-tion, deception, and untruth, as if it were a place where nothing is what it seems to be and where hypostats therefore cannot have the full color of solidity. In "The Shape of the Sword" he calls Ireland "a bitter and dear mythology" (*F*, 131; *Lab.*, 68; *Fic.*, 118)—a place of circular towers and red marshes.

Moon's betrayal of his friend comes at the end of nine days in the place where they are living. The friend, on realizing Moon has sold him out, chases Moon through corridors that give a brief suggestion of a labyrinth, to the vertiginous upper reaches of stairways; and here the syntax is noteworthy: "black corridors of nightmare and . . . deep stairwells of dizziness" (*F*, 134–135; *Lab.*, 71; *Fic.*, 122). It is as if the chase took place in a dreaming mind. One may wonder, in fact, whether this story does not actually describe one man's inner struggle against his other self and the final victory of his cowardly side.

There is not much to be said, from the standpoint of the motif, about "Theme of the Traitor and the Hero." There is Borgesian oxymoron in "gray hill" (*cerro gris*) and "red swamps" (*ciénagas rojas*), which in this context seem to have a special and subtle value. The image of a statue standing on a gray hill among red marshes assigns more color (reality) to the broad marshes than to the eminent terrain or the statue. (Hills serve a dual purpose at times; they can represent hypostats when they rise above plains or marshes, and they can also be the background for sharper hypostatizations). Perhaps this indicates that after the death of the traitor-hero Kilpatrick, his heroism is more a part of the land and its spirit than of Kilpatrick; and in the real-life context of the story, this is true. The dual reality that was Kilpatrick does not finally prevail; his single image, his illusion, does.

Kilpatrick is discovered by a few intimates to be a traitor to the Irish cause. But because the people worship him, his execution is carried out under the guise of an assassination—with his cooperation. His death is prefigured symbolically in false reports of the burning of a circular tower in his home county. Like most hypostats, he dies of a bullet; the two sudden effusions of blood (*F*, 141; *Lab.*, 75; *Fic.*, 127) no doubt signify the death (ideal reduction) of his double self, traitor and hero. Although he is already revered, Kilpatrick becomes a hero only in the act of dying—dying willingly for the cause. This is an atonement for his act of betrayal. Thus, while one hypostat is palpably destroyed, another is created:

the one which volunteers to surrender its being does so in order to preserve its image. On the ideal plane this can be conceived only as the image of an idea; logically, an uncrowned Gestalt. An idea is a Gestalt with a crowning hypostat; the image of an idea must be the condition prior to this: a Gestalt with a vacancy where the name belongs—the suggestion of something unnamed, only connoted; in other words, a symbol in Valéry's sense, a myth, or simply the "pregnant situation" again.

To make this clearer, we can look at it this way: Kilpatrick's fate is an event which "redeemed him and . . . lost him" (F, 141; Lab., 75; Fic., 126) at the same time. To redeem Kilpatrick would be to excuse him; this cannot be done, for he would be untrustworthy like Moon. To "lose" him would be to kill him publicly as a traitor, which would jeopardize the Irish cause and injure those around him. But by having him assassinated with his consent, his "esthetic fact" is preserved; he remains spiritually present while physically absent. In the terminology of the ideal, to "lose" Kilpatrick would be to "burn" him out of the mental universe (the reports of the burning tower were false, it turned out). To "redeem" him would be to transmute him into a dogma—to glorify him ultimately. The compromise, his voluntary disappearance, transforms this palpable figment, Kilpatrick, into a less palpable being that cannot be destroyed because it is now only suggested.

Although this interpretation is a bit abstruse, it is consistent with a theory of symbolism that Borges is intimately aware of. This is shown, perhaps, in that Ryan, the descendant of Kilpatrick who happens upon the truth, decides not to reveal it. The order for Kilpatrick's execution, which Kilpatrick signed himself, is still in existence, but the name of the condemned traitor has been deleted (F, 139; Lab., 74; Fic., 125). Ryan, a good Symbolist, apparently, will not speak the word that can kill the esthetic reality.

"The Other Death"

Self-delusion is a form of repentance. It often happens that a man's desire obliterates his memory of fact and imposes itself as reality. It is typical of Borges that he projects this phenomenon outward upon the objective order and allows one man's repentance to obliterate historical fact from the minds of other men. Pedro Damián proved himself a coward at Masoller in 1904; he would prefer to have died there as a hero. His petition to God for this boon is heard, but even God cannot change the past. So God changes the memory of the past. But this takes time, because every event has its infinite consequences. God has to start at the present and work backward to the event, as in Herbert Quain's novel. Finally the deed is accomplished. Between the time of old Damián's death of lung congestion and the following winter, the men who remember his cowardice and his subsequent long life have forgotten both, and they now remember only that Damián died at nineteen years of age at the battle of Massoller—a hero.

Again we are involved in the creation of a myth. It is not Damián's physical death that carries with it the symbols of the Zahir, but his imaginary or ideal death—the heroism with which his being is finally equated:

It was about four in the afternoon. On the crest of the hill the red infantry had gained strength. . . . Damián was in the forefront, yelling, and a bullet caught him full in the chest. He pulled up short in the stirrups, finished the yell, rolled to the ground and came to rest among the horses' hooves (A, 57).

The thing that was left after Kilpatrick died was a myth, an esthetic fact; the thing that is left here is simply the memory of a man (an idea) that went down fighting. Perhaps Damián's story is in some way analogous to a common psychic fact: we often lose a conviction or idea, and after losing it we realize that it really died long before and that its persistence was only an illusion.

"The South"

Borges has said that "The South" is "perhaps my best story." Largely autobiographical, it tells the story of Juan Dahlmann, who in reality dies of septicemia in a hospital—in a fever, like Damián —but whose ideal death occurs out on the plains in a fight with a *compadrito*. The death that occurred in the hospital is only insinuated. After his feverish illness, Dahlmann goes to the country to convalesce. He rides in the same kind of coach that took him to the hospital; riding on the train toward the south, he has the feeling that he is two men (*F*, 191; *Fic.*, 170) and that he is regressing in time (*F*, 192; *Fic.*, 171); and in the general store where he is challenged to a duel, he confuses the proprietor with an employe of the hospital. As he sits reading the same book that he was reading when he received the scratch that produced septicemia, he feels that his misfortune "had been annulled" (*F*, 190; *Fic.*, 170). In the store near his ancestral home he is challenged by a ruffian and is compelled to fight to the death with a knife. The final impression left by the story is that in his fevered mind, in the hospital, Dahlmann is given the death he prefers over the one that actually comes to him. Dahlmann could have avoided fighting with the ruffian if he had not been given a knife by an ancient gaucho who is described in the same words that describe the old beggar who told the inner story in "The Man on the Threshold": "The many years had reduced and polished him as the waters do a stone or as the generations of men do a proverb" (*F*, 193; *Fic.*, 172; cf. *A*, 145). Borges at times repeats in a story or essay the exact words he has used in another.

When redness fades, when blood is shed, or when redness appears at a late hour of the day, the decline of a reality is signified or foretold. At the beginning of "The South" we learn that Dahlmann's old home, to which he will try to return later, was once red but is now faded (*F*, 187; *Fic.*, 167). As soon as we have learned this and a few other details, Dahlmann scratches his head accidentally, bleeds, and soon gets an infection. After his nearly fatal (actually, fatal) illness he is released from the hospital—at seven o'clock in the morning, "with a beginning of dizziness." The symbols betray the intention of Borges to show that Dahlmann is here being resurrected in order to give him a different death. "In the yellow light of the new day all things were coming back to him" (*F*, 190; *Fic.*, 169).

His reincarnation is complete in the next paragraph, where he goes to a café and drinks black coffee while he contemplates a cat, which lives "in the present, in the eternity of the instant." But to further signify his approaching decline, Borges speaks of a white sun that turns yellow and then red as it goes down: "Now the intolerable white sun of twelve o'clock was the yellow sun that precedes dusk and would not long delay in being red" (*F*, 191; *Fic.*, 171). The sundown effect is reinforced with other images: the train's moving shadow stretched toward the horizon, and the elemental terrain unbroken by signs of human habitation. On the "lawless landscape" there was hardly more than an occasional bull. This primal vastness was intimately Dahlmann's; it was his destiny: "Everything was vast, but at the same time was intimate and, in some way, secret."

Having arrived at a station near his old home, Dahlmann goes into a café to eat. The building used to be a deep scarlet, but now is faded, and there are horses tied in front. Inside, Dahlmann is challenged by the bully and is compelled to accept the challenge —by Destiny in the form of the old gaucho, who "was as if outside of time, in an eternity." He accepts the inevitable almost as automatically as he had accepted the necessity of walking some distance from the station; it is at this point that the symbol is given which governs the rest of the story: "The sun had already gone down, but a final brilliance exalted the living, silent plain before the night should blot it out" (*F*, 192; *Fic.*, 171).

"The Maker"

The short confessional piece entitled "The Maker," appearing at the beginning of the collection of that name (*H*, 9–11; *Dream.*, 22–23) speaks in allegorical or analogous terms of Borges' physical blindness (and perhaps of his skepticism). At the moment when darkness threatened to overwhelm the poet Homer, there came to him a memory of a long-forgotten event. What that event was does not matter here; but it was one isolated moment of time and experience which, when recalled, was somehow an answer to the meaninglessness of his future as a blind man—a small reality that in some way stood for the present reality and turned Homer's (Borges') face toward his intimate destiny with a demand for courage. When this saving memory came to him, it "shone like a coin under the rain" (*H*, 10; *Dream.*, 22).

BIBLIOGRAPHY

Works by Borges:

Antología personal. Buenos Aires: Sur, S. A., 1961.
El Aleph. Buenos Aires: Emecé Editores, S. A., 1957.
El hacedor. Buenos Aires: Emecé Editores, S. A., 1960.
Ficciones. Buenos Aires: Emecé Editores, S. A., 1956.
Historia de la eternidad. Buenos Aires: Emecé Editores, S. A., 1953.
Manual de zoología fantástica. (In collaboration with Margarita Guerrero). México: Fondo de Cultura Económica, 1957 ("Breviarios" No. 125).
Otras inquisiciones. Buenos Aires: Emecé Editores, S. A., 1960.

Translations of Borges' works:

Dreamtigers. Translated by Mildred Boyer and Harold Morland, with an Introduction by Miguel Enguídanos. Austin: University of Texas Press, 1964.
Ficciones. Edited and with a Foreword by Anthony Kerrigan, and translated by Kerrigan and others. New York: Grove Press, 1962.
Labyrinths: Selected Stories and Other Writings. Edited by Donald A. Yates and James E. Irby, translated by Irby, Yates and others, and with a Preface by André Maurois and a Foreword by Irby. New York: New Directions, 1962.
Other Inquisitions. Translated by Ruth L. C. Simms, with an Introduction by James E. Irby. Austin: University of Texas Press, 1964.
A Personal Anthology. Edited and with a Foreword by Anthony Kerrigan and translated by Kerrigan, Alastair Reid, and others. New York: Grove Press, 1967.

Works about Borges:

Note. When this book was written, two important critical works on Borges had not yet appeared: Ronald Christ's *The Narrow Act*

(New York: N. Y. University Press, 1969) and L. A. Murillo's
The Cyclical Night (Cambridge: Harvard University Press, 1968).

Acevedo de Borges, Leonor. "Propos," *L'Herne* (Spring, 1964), 9–11.

Anderson Imbert, Enrique. *Historia de la literatura hispanoamericana.*
2 vols. México: Fondo de Cultura Económica, 1964.

———. "Un cuento de Borges: 'La casa de Asterión,'" *Revista Ibero-
americana*, XXV, No. 49 (1960), 33–43.

Barrenechea, Ana María. *La expresión de la irrealidad en la obra de
Jorge Luis Borges.* México: El Colegio de México, 1957.

———. *Borges the Labyrinth Maker.* Edited and translated by Robert
Lima. New York: New York University Press, 1965.

Bioy Casares, Adolfo. "Lettres et amitiés," *L'Herne* (Spring, 1964),
12–18.

Bliven, Naomi. "Stunt Man," *The New Yorker* (August 18, 1962),
95–97.

Campos, Jorge. "Las ficciones de Borges," *Insula*, XVI, No. 175 (junio
de 1961), 11.

Capsas, Cleon W. "Charlando con Borges," *Cuadernos del viento*, No. 29
(diciembre de 1962), 457–462.

Christ, Ronald. "Jorge Luis Borges," *The Paris Review*, 40 (Winter–
Spring, 1967), 116–164.

Enguídanos, Miguel. "Imaginación y evasión en los cuentos de Jorge
Luis Borges," *Papeles de Son Armadans*, XXX (septiembre de 1958),
233–251.

———. "Introduction," *Dreamtigers.* Translated by Mildred Boyer and
Harold Morland. Austin: University of Texas Press, 1964 (published
in Spanish in *Sur*, No. 285 [noviembre–diciembre, 1963], 86–91).

Fernández Moreno, César. *Esquema de Borges.* Buenos Aires: Editorial
Perrot, 1957.

Gullón, Ricardo. "Borges y su laberinto," *Insula*, XVI, No. 175 (junio de
1961), 1.

Gutiérrez Girardot, Rafael. "Jorge Luis Borges," *Mito*, VII, Nos. 39–40
(noviembre 1961–febrero 1962), 119–125.

———. *Jorge Luis Borges: ensayo de interpretación.* Madrid: Insula,
1959.

Iduarte, Andrés. "Borges es el Aleph," *Revista Hispánica Moderna*, XX,
Nos. 1–2 (1954), 75–76.

Irby, James E. "The Structure of the Stories of Jorge Luis Borges."
Unpublished doctoral dissertation, Department of Romance Languages, University of Michigan, 1963.

——. "Introduction," *Labyrinths: Selected Stories and Other Writings*. Edited by Donald A. Yates and James E. Irby. New York: New Directions, 1962.

——. "Introduction," *Other Inquisitions*. Translated by Ruth L. C. Simms. Austin: University of Texas Press, 1964.

——. "Nota sobre 'El Aleph' y 'El Zahir,' " *Cuadernos del Viento*, No. 3 (octubre de 1960), 39–41.

Maurois, André. "Preface," *Labyrinths: Selected Stories and Other Writings*. Edited by Donald A. Yates and James E. Irby. New York: New Directions, 1962.

Mejía Duque, Jaime. "De nuevo Jorge Luis Borges," *Mito*, VII, Nos. 39–40 (noviembre 1961–febrero 1962), 129–140.

Milleret, Jean de. *Entretiens avec Jorge Luis Borges*. Paris: Editions Pierre Belfond, 1967.

Murillo, L. A. "The Labyrinths of Jorge Luis Borges: an Introductory to the Stories of *The Aleph*," *Modern Language Quarterly*, XX, No. 3 (September, 1959), 259–266.

Ríos Patrón, José Luis. *Jorge Luis Borges*. Buenos Aires: La Mandrágora, 1955.

Rodríguez Monegal, Emir. "Borges: teoría y práctica," *Número*, VI, No. 27 (diciembre de 1955), 124–157.

Tamayo, Marcial, and Ruiz-Díaz, Adolfo. *Borges, enigma y clave*. Buenos Aires: Editorial Nuestro Tiempo, 1955.

Wahl, Jean. "Les personnes et l'impersonnel," *L'Herne* (Spring, 1964), 257–264.

GENERAL WORKS ON MYTH, ESTHETICS, SYMBOLISM, AND PHILOSOPHY:

Altizer, Thomas J. J. "The Religious Meaning of Myth and Symbol," in *Truth, Myth and Symbol*. Edited by Thomas J. J. Altizer, William A. Beardslee, and J. Harvey Young. Englewood Cliffs, N. J.: Prentice-Hall, Inc., 1962 (Spectrum Book No. S–40).

Berlin, Isaiah. *The Hedgehog and the Fox*. New York: New American Library, 1957 (Mentor Book No. 198).

Bidney, David. "Myth, Symbolism and Truth," in *Myth, a Symposium*. Edited by Thomas Sebeok. Bibliographical and Special Series of the American Folklore Society, Vol. V, Philadelphia, 1955.

Bioy Casares, Adolfo. "Prólogo," *Antología de la literatura fantástica*. Edited by Jorge Luis Borges, Silvina Ocampo, and Adolfo Bioy Casares. Buenos Aires: Editorial Sudamericana, 1965 (Colección Piragua).

Breton, André. "Seconde manifeste du surréalisme," *Manifestes du surréalisme*. Paris: Gallimard, 1963 (Collection Idées).

Campbell, Joseph. "The Historical Development of Mythology," *Daedalus* (Spring, 1959), 232–254.

Cassirer, Ernst. *The Philosophy of Symbolic Forms*. Translated by Ralph Manheim, with an Introduction by Charles W. Hendel. 3 vols. New Haven: Yale University Press, 1953.

——. *Language and Myth*. Translated by Susanne K. Langer. New York: Dover Publications, 1946.

——. *An Essay on Man*. New Haven: Yale University Press, 1944.

Chase, Richard. *Quest for Myth*. Baton Rouge: Louisiana State University Press, 1949.

De Mourgues, Odette. "The European Background to Baroque Sensibility," in *From Donne to Marvell* (Vol. III of *A Guide to English Literature*). Edited by Boris Ford. Harmondsworth, Middlesex: Penguin Books, 1956 (Pelican Book No. A325).

Durant, Will. *The Story of Philosophy*. New York: The Washington Square Press, Inc., 1961.

Eliade, Mircea. *Myths, Dreams and Mysteries*. Translated by Philip Mairet. London: Harvill Press, 1960.

——. *The Myth of the Eternal Return*. Translated by Willard R. Trask. New York: Pantheon Books, 1954.

——. "The Yearning for Paradise in Primitive Tradition," *Daedalus* (Spring, 1959), 255–267.

Ferrater Mora, José. *Diccionario de filosofía*. Buenos Aires, 1958.

Frazer, Sir James George. *The New Golden Bough*. Abridged and edited with notes by Theodor H. Gaster. New York: The New American Library, 1964 (Mentor Book No. MY594).

Hatzfeld, Helmut. *Estudios literarios sobre misticismo español*. Madrid: Editorial Gredos, 1955.

Langer, Susanne K. *Philosophy in a New Key*. New York: The New American Library, 1948 (Mentor Book No. MD101).

——. *Feeling and Form*. New York: Charles Scribner's Sons, 1953.

Lewis, C. S. "Preface," *George Macdonald: an Anthology*. Garden City, N. Y.: Doubleday and Company, 1962 (Dolphin Book No. C373).

Malinowski, Bronislaw. *Magic, Science and Religion and Other Essays*. Garden City, N. Y.: Doubleday and Company, 1948 (Anchor Book No. A23).

Murray, Henry A. "Introduction," *Daedalus* (Spring, 1959, issue on "Myth and Mythmaking"), 211–222.

Paz, Octavio. *El laberinto de la soledad.* 4th ed. México: Fondo de Cultura Económica, 1964.

——. *The Labyrinth of Solitude.* Translated by Lysander Kemp. New York: Grove Press, 1961.

Pope, M. H. "Number, Numbering, Numbers," in *The Interpreter's Dictionary of the Bible.* 4 vols. New York: Abingdon Press, 1962.

Raymond, Marcel. *From Baudelaire to Surrealism.* Translated by "G.M.," with a Preface by Robert Motherwell, an Introduction by Harold Rosenberg, and a Bibliography by Bernard Karpel (Vol. X of *The Documents of Modern Art*) New York: Wittenborn, Schulz, Inc., 1950.

Rodó, José Enrique. *Ariel.* Tercera edición. México: Espasa-Calpe Mexicana, 1963 (Colección Austral).

Schorer, Mark. "The Necessity of Myth," *Daedalus* (Spring, 1959), 359–362.

Scranton, Robert L. "Myth in Myth," in *Truth, Myth and Symbol.* Edited by Thomas J. J. Altizer, William A. Beardslee, and J. Harvey Young. Englewood Cliffs, N. J.: Prentice-Hall, Inc., 1962 (Spectrum Book No. S–40).

Shattuck, Roger. *The Banquet Years.* New York: Doubleday and Company, 1961 (Anchor Book No. A238).

Sypher, Wylie. *Rococo to Cubism in Art and Literature.* New York: Random House, 1963 (Vintage Book No. V–299).

Tillich, Paul. *The Courage to Be.* New Haven: Yale University Press, 1952.

——. *The Dynamics of Faith.* New York: Harper and Brothers, 1958.

Tindall, William York. *The Literary Symbol.* Bloomington: Indiana University Press, 1955.

Tovar, F. Gil. "Hacia una psicología barroca," in *El Tiempo* (Bogotá), 15 diciembre 1963 ("Lecturas dominicales," 5).

Urban, Wilbur M. *Language and Reality.* London: George Allen and Unwin, Ltd., 1939.

Vaihinger, Hans. *The Philosophy of 'As If.'* Translated by C. K. Ogden. London: Routledge and Kegan Paul, Ltd., 1924.

Valéry, Paul. *Oeuvres.* Edited by Jean Hytier. Paris: Gallimard, 1957.

Vignoli, Tito. *Myth and Science.* New York: D. Appleton and Co., 1882.

Watts, Alan. *Myth and Ritual in Christianity.* New York: Grove Press, 1960.

Wellek, René, and Warren, Austin. *Theory of Literature.* New York: Harcourt, Brace and World, Inc., 1956 (Harvest Book No. HB22).

Printed in the USA
CPSIA information can be obtained
at www.ICGtesting.com
LVHW041142310824
789807LV00001B/17